Starting with Sheep

A Beginner's Guide

Mary Castell

Broad Leys Publishing

Starting with Sheep

First Edition: 2000

Copyright © 2000 Mary Castell

Published by Broad Leys Publishing Company

Printed by Design & Print

A catalogue record for this book is available from the British Library.

ISBN 906137 28 4

Outside front cover: Icelandic Ram. Photograph by Laura Densmore

Dedication
To Paul, Martin, Chris and Bernard
for their kindly tolerance of the sheep.

Acknowledgments
I would like to thank Caroline Key for sharing her expertise and enthusiasm, and Philippa Tristram and Daphne Child for their helpful suggestions when reading the manuscript.
I would also like to thank Katie and David Thear for having given me the opportunity to write about sheep.

For details of other publications please contact the publishers:
Broad Leys Publishing Company,
Buriton House, Station Road,
Newport, Saffron Walden,
Essex CB11 3PL, England.
Tel: 01799 540922
Fax: 01799 541367
E-mail: info@countrysmallholding.com
Website: www.countrysmallholding.com

Contents

Sheep are quiet, docile animals whose only protection is flight or seeking refuge in a flock.
Photo: Katie Thear

Preface

This book is written with three objects in mind. First: to help those who think that they might like to keep sheep but wish to know what this would involve. Second: to assist would-be sheep-keepers to make their initial decisions; how many sheep to keep, what sort of sheep, and how much land and equipment they will need. Third: to provide new shepherds with a clear and concise guide to help them in the early years of sheep-keeping.

The book describes the tasks involved in sheep husbandry, and provides information as to when and how to carry them out. The behaviour of sheep is explained, and at every stage suggestions are made as to how new shepherds can avoid difficulties by working with the natural instincts of their sheep.

(Mary Castell)

Introduction

"It profiteth the lord to have discreet shepherds, watchful and kindly, so that the sheep be not tormented by their wrath but crop their pasture in peace and joyfulness; for it is a token of the shepherd's kindness if the sheep be not scattered abroad but browse around him in company. (Walter of Henley, early 13th century).

Sheep are quiet, docile animals. Their only protection against predators is flight, or seeking refuge in numbers, which they achieve by forming a flock. These characteristics make them easy to control, and led to the domestication of wild sheep in Asia over 10,000 years ago. During the centuries sheep have adapted to widely varying environments. There are types of sheep that can survive on mountains, on exposed islands, or even in semi-desert conditions. Man has added to this variety by breeding sheep which produce more milk and lambs, have longer or finer wool, or larger carcases. This has led to the large number of sheep breeds which we find today.

The adaptability of the sheep, its easy handling, and value as a producer of wool, meat and milk, have made it one of the most common farm animals. The same factors lead smallholders to make sheep one of their first acquisitions. The wide variety of breeds available is also an attraction. Small or very docile breeds can be chosen if the handler is not particularly strong, or wishes to involve children in the care of the animals. For those interested in crafts, there is a wide range of fleece types and colours. Sheep are modest in their requirements. Good stock fencing is needed but little equipment is required. Housing is not necessary, though it is useful to have a shed available at lambing time or for sick animals.

The amount of time a flock owner devotes to his sheep varies with the seasons. For over half the year fifteen minutes per day and a few hours at weekends is sufficient time to devote to a small flock. A breeding flock requires more observation during the mating period, and very frequent visits and considerable time spent with the flock during the three months that cover late pregnancy, lambing and the period when the lambs are young. Walter of Henley's advice, given above, is excellent. The work involved in caring for the flock will be lighter, and the experience more rewarding, if the shepherd knows his sheep well enough to notice unusual behaviour, and the sheep trust him sufficiently to be co-operative.

This book aims to make the first years of sheep-keeping enjoyable and unproblematic. *Part I* is concerned with the foundation of a small flock. Various systems of sheep-keeping are described, breeds and their characteristics are listed, and the equipment and area of land required are considered. *Part II* includes a calendar describing the care that sheep require throughout the year, and chapters on feeding sheep and the treatment of common infections. *Part III* addresses the care of a breeding flock from mating in the autumn, to lambing in the spring and shearing, weaning, and marketing of lambs and wool in the summer. A reference section includes a summary of current *Government Regulations.*

Part 1 Preliminary Decisions

Chapter 1 Sheep-keeping Systems

A neighbour's sheep in your paddock

Some people acquire sheep largely by accident. Perhaps they move to a house which happens to have a paddock, and a friend suggests that they buy a few sheep to keep the grass mown; or perhaps the paddock is for a pony and someone advises them to get a few sheep to keep the grazing in good order. This is good advice concerning the grazing, nevertheless it is unwise to go out and buy a couple of sheep before one knows what is involved in their care. The most simple solution is to find someone who is looking for grazing for a few sheep. Farmers and smallholders often need small paddocks to supplement their grazing in the winter, or to keep rams away from the ewes. Local Smallholders' Groups, Rare Breeds Support Groups or local farmers may know of someone looking for grazing for sheep, and, failing these, a short advertisement at your local feed merchant's should bring a response.

When letting or lending grazing you will need to provide secure stock fencing (electric fencing is unreliable), secure gates and probably a water source. Once you have sheep in your field you will soon discover if you enjoy their presence. When you can tell them apart, and know enough of their behaviour to notice that one is behaving strangely, and take this seriously enough to phone the owner, you will have learnt the most important step in sheep husbandry, namely how to look at sheep. Should you decide to acquire your own flock, further decisions will have to be made, the main one being whether it is to be a breeding or non-breeding flock.

A non-breeding flock

A non-breeding flock is suitable for those who wish to own a few sheep but cannot devote the time and labour necessary for a breeding flock. These may be spinners, weavers and felters who wish to possess some sheep with interesting fleeces, or paddock owners who wish to become involved with their woolly mowers or raise a few bought-in lambs for the freezer. A non-breeding flock can consist of females that are not put to the ram or wethers, ie, castrated males that the breeder intended for the butcher. Wethers are a good choice because they are more docile than rams and easier to handle but their wool is as fine as that of ewes. Wethers can be bought from flocks specialising in wool production for the price of a butch-

Fig. 1.1 Fleeces in varied colours add attraction and value to a small flock.
Photo: Mary Castell

er's lamb, which is considerably less than that of a breeding ewe. A further advantage is that it is easy to keep a flock of mixed breeds as long as the sheep are similar in size to avoid bullying. Another possibility is to buy a few lambs to fatten for the freezer. They will keep the paddock well mown during the summer months and by the time grass growth is declining they should be ready for the butcher.

The care of a non-breeding flock is simple because the health complications and extra care and feeding associated with lambing are avoided. An experienced sheep-keeper should be able to give you sufficient instruction to enable you to undertake day-to-day care, and should be able to offer advice if the sheep appear sick or listless. You should walk through the sheep paddock every day to make sure that they are well and have not suffered any mishaps, such as becoming tangled up in brambles. Sheep infections spread rapidly so should be treated before the whole flock is affected. In addition to this a few hours once a week should be sufficient to keep the paddock in order and carry out the husbandry tasks listed in *Chapter 4*. Grazing should be adequate for these sheep for most of the year. From Christmas until the grass starts to grow again, they may require hay, and in bad weather a few nuts or a feed block. When you are away a well informed friend is needed to carry out the daily check and call the vet when required.

A breeding flock

A breeding flock involves spending considerably more time on supervision, feeding and management. It is advisable to attend a lambing course because it is not fair to ask a neighbour to let you experiment on his sheep. The bills from the feed merchant and vet will be larger, and more equipment will be required. Holidays cannot be taken from six weeks pre-lambing until the lambing season is over, and it is unwise to be absent during mating. On the other hand the excitement and satisfaction of breeding healthy lambs, and the delight of watching them at play, is worth a great deal.

The ewes

It is best to begin with a small number of 'middle aged' ewes, perhaps three or four which already lambed a few times. Starting a flock in this way has several advantages. Older ewes will not be as expensive as young stock; you will soon be able to tell them apart; they should be easier to handle; and at lambing will be experienced mothers. Moreover, when you come to buy other sheep, you will already possess a group of ewes which will act as leaders because they are accustomed to you, your farm and your routine. Do not buy bottle fed lambs! They may be difficult to handle and have health problems.

The ram

The acquisition of a ram is best avoided in the first year. Keeping your own ram is not without complications. Even a quiet, elderly fellow will become more aggressive in the autumn as the breeding season approaches, and must be kept in a secure place, out of sight of the females and well away from them. He will need a companion but will probably fight with a ram of his own size, so a ram lamb or wether is a good choice.

Some rams are especially aggressive and may kill another ram. In my experience horned rams are not more aggressive than polled rams, but when they fight can inflict more serious injuries.

To avoid keeping a ram in your first year, your first sheep can be bought in the autumn already in lamb; alternatively you can ask the breeder of the ewes if you may hire a ram for the first season or take your ewes to his ram. Where grazing is limited it may be advisable to hire or borrow a ram every year. Not only are the problems associated with in-breeding and the difficulties of keeping a ram avoided, but a different ram can be hired each year, which allows experiments in crossing to produce interesting fleeces or larger lambs for the freezer. It is not difficult to hire a ram because breeders like to keep several rams of different blood lines, and often have a couple which are not working or have already covered the ewes. Since these rams will be strangers on your holding they will require extra supervision and may need to be insured while they are on loan. This can be arranged through a firm specialising in rural insurance.

Preparing to chose a breed

This is the next decision to be made, and is pleasurable but not easy, because of the large number of British breeds and Continental breeds available. Some sheep are very attractive and their lambs exceedingly appealing, so it is very wise to be clear of what you want from your sheep *before* you go to shows to look at them. Buying on impulse may result in acquiring a breed which is too difficult to handle; not adapted to the environment in which you live; has wool unsuited to the craft which interests you; or a carcase that matures too slowly for your needs.

The following paragraphs are designed to assist the prospective buyer in drawing up a list of breeds which are *unsuitable* for him or for his objectives in keeping sheep, and which he has made a firm decision *not* to buy.

Handling

The first decision must be to exclude any breed which is too large or too heavy for the new shepherd to handle on his own. Sheep appear to get heavier as the shepherd gets older, so this must be borne in mind, as must possible injury to children from horned or heavy breeds.

Environmental considerations

The next step is to think very seriously of excluding any breed which is unsuited to your area.

Hill breeds

Hill breeds have light bodies and specialised fleeces which enable them to live on hills and mountains where the grazing is poor, there is little or no shelter, and they are exposed to high humidity. They are used to grazing very large areas, do not take kindly to being fenced in, and are very good at escaping. They are used to drinking running water from a stream, and are not used to being fed by man, so have problems adapting to a water trough, a bucket of nuts and a hay rack.

If you live in the lowlands and decide that you must have a hill breed, do not buy them from a mountain farm, but from a breeder living in a location similar to your own, and make sure that your fencing is secure. If these sheep cannot go over, they will go under.

Lowland breeds

Lowland breeds need good grazing to support their heavy bodies, and their wool is not resistant to fog, mists, and heavy rain. A lowland sheep kept on a hill farm requires housing during bad weather and probably at lambing, and also considerable extra feeding in the form of hay and concentrates.

A commercial flock producing meat lambs

There are further limitations on the choice of those wishing to start a small commercial flock. There will be only a certain number of breeds or cross-breds that find buyers in the local market, and the local abattoir will have a preference for the size and weight of carcases they handle. Most commercial meat lambs are out of cross-bred ewes by a meat-sheep sire, the cross-bred ewes are usually bought in, as are the rams.

Most smallholders are well advised to keep pure bred ewes and buy a good meat ram. The best course of action is to visit your local market to see which sheep are popular, talk to farming neighbours and your local butchers, and then make your choice among the breeds they favour.

Experienced farmers often have difficulty in making a profit, so the production of meat lambs should be considered with care. Moreover smallholders with limited land may find that their grazing is insufficient from mid-summer onwards to support the ewes and those lambs still too light to be sold for meat. These lambs will have to be sold as 'store lambs', that is lambs that are sold to other farmers for fattening. These buyers are unwilling to give a reasonable price for any breed which they do not know, because they cannot estimate the time the lamb is likely to take to reach an acceptable weight.

Sheep for wool, sheepskins, and meat for home consumption

When this is the object a wide choice of breeds is possible. Talking to members of the local spinners' group will give some idea of the type of fleeces they prefer, with the proviso that what spinners consider to be a wonderful fleece one year, they may not buy the next, because they wish to try something new.

Sheepskins fetch above average prices if they are attractively coloured, or have lustrous or curly wool *(Fig. 1.1)*. The cost of tanning is considerable, and home tanning laborious, which makes the return on the sale of small skins, or ordinary white sheepskins, unattractive.

Fig. 1.2 Visit as many sheep shows as you can before making a choice.
Photo: Royal Agricultural Society of England.

Making a choice

My advice is to go to as many sheep shows as you can. *(Fig. 1.2).* Rare and Minority Breed shows are excellent because such a wide variety of sheep are on display, while local agricultural shows are a good place to see the best of the sheep native to your area. When talking to breeders remember that they are enthusiasts, and consider their breed the most docile, the best tasting and altogether the most outstanding in the land.

Further information on any breed that attracts your attention can be obtained from the *Breed Society Secretary* who can be contacted through the *National Sheep Association.* Since you will spend many hours over many years caring for your sheep, the main consideration is that you should like the breed you choose, but keep rigidly to your exclusion list.

Buying your sheep

Once you have collected information about possible breeds, discuss this with friends who keep other breeds and can give impartial advice. When you have settled on a breed visit several breeders, and if possible take a friend who knows about sheep, as he will be able to tell if the animals are in good physical condition, and on this basis advise you on which individuals to buy. Only buy at a sale if you are certain that the sheep comes from a healthy flock. Any sheep you consider should stand squarely upon strong, straight legs, and should have healthy feet. Shoulders should be strong and wide, and the back long and level with the spinal bones just detectable. Udders of ewes must be without lumps and the testicles of rams a good size and firm. The mouth of the sheep should be inspected carefully to ascertain if the incisors meet the upper pad at a right angle; if they slope forward or back the animal must be rejected as it cannot graze effectively. This is also the case when teeth are missing.

Chapter 2 Sheep Breeds

Breeds are different types of sheep which man has produced, either directly by selective breeding, or indirectly by introducing them to new environments to which they have adapted. All sheep descend from the wild sheep of Asia, which were domesticated about 12,000 years ago in Iran/Iraq. Wild sheep are mainly brown in colour, with some black and white markings. They have very large horns, usually in both sexes, are slender and long-legged, and carry a very fine coat of underwool and an outer coat of coarse kemp fibres. Primitive breeds still resemble their wild ancestors in some respects.

Describing sheep

The adult male sheep is known as a *ram* or *tup*; mating is called *tupping*. A *terminal sire* refers to a ram from a meat breed which is used to produce good meat lambs from ewes of other breeds. A *wether* is a castrated male. The female is a *ewe*. The young up to six months of age or till one year are *ram* or *tup lambs*, and *ewe lambs*. A *shearling* is a sheep that has been shorn once. There are many local names for sheep, for instance *tegs*, *hogs* and *hoggets* are aged between six months and one year, *theaves* and *gimmers* are young ewes aged over one year.

Size is expressed by giving the average weight of a ram and ewe, the ram being heavier.

Prolificacy is the number of lambs a ewe is likely to bear, given as a percentage of lambs in a flock per ewe. A flock of 100 mountain ewes could have a percentage of under 100 (= one lamb per ewe and a few not lambing). A flock run on better hill land might produce 120% (= majority singles, some twins). The Lleyn, a very prolific breed, has a percentage of 200 or even over. The average Lleyn ewe is expected to produce twins and sometimes triplets.

Wool is described by the length, called *length of staple*; the average fleece **weight**; and the **fineness,** expressed in the diameter in *microns* (1 micron = one millionth of a meter), or the *Bradford Count*, a *Wool Board* measurement of fineness. For example, the Shetland sheep, a fine woolled breed, has a fibre measurement varying between 23 - 33 microns. The Bradford Count is 50 to 60, where the higher number represents the finer wool.

Small flocks and commercial flocks compared

There is a significant difference between the system followed by a small flock owner or smallholder, and the system which has been adopted by the majority of commercial farmers. The small flock owner usually keeps pure-bred sheep, while the commercial system relies upon the use of cross-breeding and the purchase of ewe replacements.

The small flock owner

The small flock owner usually chooses a breed which attracts him and increases the size of his flock by keeping his ewe lambs. Occasionally he buys a new ram of the same breed to avoid in-breeding, and, in years when he does not intend to keep any ewe lambs, he may hire a meat ram to improve the lambs that are to go for slaughter. He may make a certain amount by selling attractive sheepskins and speciality wools to hand spinners.

The commercial farmer

The commercial farmer in the mountains breeds his own ewes and rams but most of his ewes are sold when they are three or four years old to farmers on somewhat lower land. These commercial farmers specialise in producing hardy, large and prolific cross-bred ewes by putting the mountain ewes to a ram from a large prolific breed. These ewes are bought by lowland commercial farmers who cross them with heavy meat rams, acquired from another breeder, and all the lambs produced are sold to the butcher. This system is known as *stratification* because it makes use of the genetic diversity of sheep from the mountains, uplands and lowlands. The system also benefits from the hybrid vigour induced by crossing. At the time of writing, wool and sheepskins do not represent a significant part of a commercial sheep farmer's return.

Rare breeds

These are breeds in which numbers have fallen to such an extent that they have been close to extinction. They are on the lists of the *Rare Breeds Survival Trust* which monitors their progress and gives advice and encouragement to breeders. The breeds are divided into *Rare Breeds*, which are placed in different classes mainly according to rarity, and the *Minority Breeds*, in which numbers have increased but are still low enough to require monitoring by the Trust.

Rare breeds can be divided into two groups according to the reason for their rarity. The first group are the *primitives* which in general are not commercially viable. They resemble breeds kept in Britain in pre-Roman times, have some characteristics in common with wild sheep, and are small.

The second group consists of *more modern breeds which have fallen out of favour with commercial farmers*, perhaps because a breed produces too large a carcase for today's market. Sometimes, as circumstances alter, their special qualities become useful again, causing their numbers to increase rapidly. In the breed lists below (R) is placed after rare and minority breeds.

Dairy sheep

These are breeds producing large quantities of milk, which is mainly made into cheese, but also yoghurt and ice cream. Because of their milkiness they are able to rear twins and triplets without difficulty, hence are highly prolific. Some of the old dairy breeds of Britain, which were used to produce cheese, such as the **Lleyn** and **Wensleydale**, have found a new place in commercial sheep production as the sires of prolific crossbred ewes. Today the **Dutch Friesland**, and to a lesser extent the **Dorset Horn**, are the main breeds used in the small British sheep dairying industry.

British breeds

The following paragraphs list the traditional British breeds. Breeds developed from British breeds during the past 60 years are omitted as are almost all imports from the Continent.

Scottish breeds

Scotland boasts the most numerous British sheep breed, the **Scottish Blackface**, a horned hill sheep, with a shaggy coat, which protects the animal from high humidity. It is only absent in part of the Borders and the Lowlands of the north east, where the **Cheviot** is preferred. This is a white faced sheep with a heavier body and finer, closer fleece than the Blackface. Scotland is also home to all but one of our native primitive breeds, see below.

Primitive breeds, including the Jacob and the Gotland

Primitive breeds are very ancient and still resemble wild sheep in many respects. The **Soay** (R) is a very small brown sheep and is the most primitive. It represents the sheep kept by the earliest farmers and we are lucky that it survived in a feral state on one of the islands of the St. Kilda group. There are now flocks throughout the country and colours other than brown are known.

The **Boreray** (R), from the same islands, represents a less primitive breed. The **North Ronaldsay** (R) from the Orkneys, the **Shetland** (R) (*Fig. 2.1*) and the **Icelandic** are closely related. They are found in all the natural colours and many patterns. The North Ronaldsay is well known because it lives on seaweed; the Shetland boasts a very fine fleece; and the rather larger Icelandic has a dual fleece of fine underwool and long outer hairs.

The **Hebridean** (R) is a small black sheep which sometimes has four horns. This is also true of the **Manx Loghtan** (R) from the Isle of Man, which is brown.

The **Castlemilk Moorit** (R) from south west Scotland was bred about one hundred years ago from a Soay, Mouflon, Manx cross.

The **Jacob** and **Gotland** are not primitive but are included here because they

14

are difficult to classify. The Jacob *(Fig. 2.5)* is a well known piebald sheep which may have two or four horns and probably originated in Portugal or Spain. It is prolific and carries a good fleece much favoured by hand spinners. The Gotland is a grey sheep from Sweden which has a lustrous, curly coat and is used for sheepskin jackets as well as wool.

Welsh sheep and the Clun

Wales is home to a large number of breeds. By far the most numerous is the **Welsh Mountain** *(Fig. 2.2)* of which there are several types varying from the small, often tan faced sheep of Snowdonia and the high hills, to the larger, white faced animals found on the lower slopes, and in South Wales. Medium sized breeds, less closely related to the Welsh Mountain, are found in central Wales. These include the **Beulah Speckled Face**, the **Welsh Hill Speckled Face**, the **Brecknock Hill Cheviot**, the **Hill Radnor** (R), and the **Kerry Hill** (R).

The **Clun** is a prolific medium sized breed from Shropshire, just over the border from the territory of the Kerry Hill.

West Wales is home to the **Llanwenog** (R), an attractive, black faced and prolific sheep (mature ewes 180%), while the most prolific of these breeds (over 200%) is the **Lleyn,** from the peninsula of that name in north west Wales. In recent years the Lleyn, once registered as a rare breed, has become popular as a producer of crossbred ewes.

Wales has retained a group of naturally coloured sheep which are of interest to the producer of wool for the craft market. The **Black Welsh Mountain** is completely black, while the **Balwen Welsh Mountain** (R) is black with a white stripe down the nose, white feet and white on the bottom half of the tail. The **Badger Face Welsh Mountain** comes in two types; the **Torddu** has black stripes above the eyes and a black stripe which runs from under the chin to the belly and continues the length of the underside of the tail; the **Torwen** has the reverse colouring with a smaller eye stripe.

Sheep of the Pennines and Lake District

The **Swaledale** is the dominant Hill Breed kept on the exposed Pennines and is related to the other Pennine breeds. It is horned and has a shaggy coat and partially black face. The **Dalesbred** and **Rough Fell** are similar breeds from the western Pennines.

The **Lonk**, the **Derbyshire Gritstone** and the **White Faced Woodland** (R) are larger Pennine breeds with finer wool.

The Lake District is home to an unique grey sheep, the **Herdwick,** which is probably Norse in origin. The fleece consists of a fine undercoat and exceedingly coarse outer coat which enables it to survive on the mountains.

Fig. 2.1 Shetland ram. *Photo: British Wool Marketing Board.*

Fig. 2.2 Welsh Mountain ram. *Photo: British Wool Marketing Board.*

Breeds of the South-West

This group is remarkable for the diversity of breeds which arose from only two main types, the *white-faced shortwools* and the *lustre longwools*. The **Portland** (R) is the most ancient breed in the first group. It is a small sheep with tan face and legs; the lambs are born a foxy red. The horns are heavily spiralled showing Merino influence. The **Dorset Horn** (there is also a polled type) is a medium sized, well muscled sheep, with a fine fleece. It also shows Merino influence, not only in the horns but also in its ability to produce lambs throughout the year. These qualities make it a popular producer of out-of-season meat lambs.

The **Wiltshire Horn** (R) has developed into a hardy meat breed without wool. It is covered by a short, sparse, hairy coat, with a very short fine undercoat which moults in the spring. In contrast two other hardy sheep in this group, the **Exmoor Horn** and the **Devon Closewool**, carry a dense fleece of fine wool. The second group consists of polled sheep; the **Grey Faced Dartmoor** (R), the **White Faced Dartmoor** (R) and the **Devon and Cornwall Longwool** *(Fig. 2.3)*. All three produce heavy fleeces of long, curly, lustre wool. The two Dartmoor breeds are good medium sized sheep, the Devon and Cornwall Longwool is a heavy breed.

The Longwools

These breeds have been strongly influenced by breeding programmes carried out in the eighteenth century to provide larger sheep with heavier fleeces and better carcases. Some of these breeds are not suitable for today's market and have become rare, others play an important part as the sires of crossbred ewes. Two breeds with a long history, the **Cotswold** (R) and **Romney** from Kent, both with medium length wool, are connected to this group because they may have played a part in the very early development of the longwools. The Cotswold was 'improved' in size in the nineteenth century but became unpopular when large joints went out of fashion. The Romney combines a heavy fleece with a good carcase, and is still kept in very large numbers both here and abroad.

The **Leicester Longwool** (R), **Lincoln** (R), **Teeswater**(R) and **Wensleydale** (R) are very large sheep with exceptionally long lustrous wool. Though they all registered as Rare Breeds they are still used as sires for crossbred ewes. The **Blue Faced Leicester** has wool which is very curly, fine and dense, and commands a high price. This is a very prolific breed and the most popular sire for crossbred ewes. The **Border Leicester** is also prolific and, as a sire for crossbred ewes, comes second in popularity.

The Down Breeds, the Norfolk Horn and the Ryeland

Down breeds are short woolled meat sheep which were developed from the old Southdown and other local breeds in the early nineteenth century. The black-

Fig. 2.5 A line up of Jacobs at an agricultural show. *Photo: Katie Thear*

headed **Suffolk** is the most popular native terminal sire, largely due to the rapid growth of the crossbred lambs. The Suffolk was the result of an accidental cross between a Southdown and the old wool sheep of East Anglia, the **Norfolk Horn** (R), which was only just rescued from extinction by a complicated breeding programme. Other Down breeds, such as the **Hampshire Down** *(Fig. 2.4)*, the **Dorset Down** (R), the **Shropshire** (R) and **Oxford Down** (R, very large), have suffered from competition with continental terminal sires. Two smaller fine woolled breeds, the **Southdown** (R) and the **Ryeland** (R), are used to cover ewes of the smaller breeds.

Continental breeds

Many breeds, mainly meat breeds, have been imported from the Continent in recent years. The two outstanding terminal sires have been the Dutch **Texel** and the French **Charollais**. The small sheep dairying sector has made a practice of importing the outstandingly milky **Friesland** from Holland.

Addresses and telephone numbers of breed society secretaries can be obtained from the *National Sheep Association.*

Information on breeders of naturally occurring coloured strains of normally white sheep, e.g. black or grey Wensleydale, can be obtained from the *British Coloured Sheep Breeders' Association.*

Fig. 2.3 Devon and Cornwall Longwool ram. *Photo: British Wool Marketing Board.*

Fig. 2.4 Hampshire Down ram. *Photo: British Wool Marketing Board.*

Chapter 3   Grazing, Handling Systems and Housing

Grazing

First it is necessary to consider the *stocking rate*, that is the number of sheep that can be kept to one acre of pasture. This is difficult to determine because there are so many variables. These include:

• *Size of the breed*: large sheep need more grazing of better quality than small sheep, and their feet do more damage to the sward.

• *Location of the holding*: the growing season of grass is shorter in the north and on high ground.

• *Soil type*: some land dries out in summer, other land becomes boggy in winter, some land is fertile and some very poor.

• *Housing*: where sheep can be kept inside from January to March damage to the new grass buds is prevented and the grazing considerably improved.

In general it is wise to consult your neighbours as to the fertility of your land, and possibly have a soil test carried out to ascertain if there are any mineral deficiencies which may affect the sheep. In any event keep only four or six ewes in the first year, increase numbers gradually and remember that all your first six ewes may produce twins, resulting in a flock of eighteen in six months time!

Sub-dividing the pasture

Sheep are subject to stomach worms and do poorly on dirty grass. Dividing the pasture into a minimum of three paddocks and circulating the sheep every couple of weeks avoids the pasture becoming so contaminated with droppings that the grass is unpalatable to the sheep, and becomes so infested with intestinal worms that it is a health hazard. This need not be expensive as electric fencing can be used. Regular worming of both ewes and lambs is necessary on restricted grazing. Farmers avoid these problems by alternating their grazing between cattle and sheep, and by using the *aftermath* (new grass that springs up after the hay has been cut) as grazing for weaned lambs.

Improved pasture describes land that has been ploughed and re-seeded with modern, improved grass seed. These fields are suitable for the heavier breeds of sheep which require a lot of feed. *Un-improved pasture* contains a greater variety of grasses, and also herbs and weeds which have deeper roots and contain more minerals. Mountain and Primitive sheep seek out the weeds and herbs, and do well on this type of grazing.

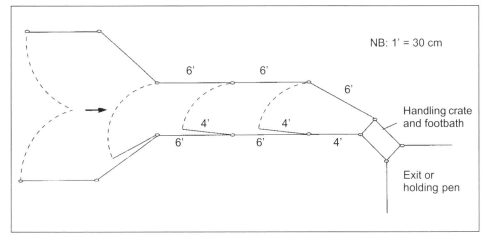

Fig. 3.1 A simple handling system

Fencing

Secure *boundary fencing and gates* must be provided to protect the owner's garden, the neighbour's land, the sheep from straying dogs, and to prevent animals escaping onto the road. The most satisfactory fencing for this purpose is constructed from stock netting 800 mm in width, topped by two strands of barbed wire, the top strand being 200 mm above the netting. The fence is supported on wooden posts around 100 mm thick and approximately 3 metres apart. The netting has narrower apertures at the bottom to prevent small lambs escaping. Lambs from Primitive and Hill breeds sometimes try to escape by burrowing and can be deterred by fixing a strand of barbed wire at ground level. *Internal fencing* can be of a lighter construction.

Electric fencing is often used internally because it can be moved easily. Gates can be constructed from hurdles. Electric fencing can be in the form of netting or wires supported by plastic stakes, and can be run from the mains or from a battery powered unit. It needs to be inspected regularly, especially in wet or windy weather, to see that it is not shorting out on herbage, bits of twig etc., and it cannot operate in snow. It is wise to introduce lambs to electric fencing when they are very young so that they learn to avoid it. Electric netting can be unsatisfactory for horned breeds.

Hedges are not ideal for sheep. Long woolled animals may get caught in them and some breeds, especially the Primitives, are fond of eating hedges and try to push their way through gaps. It may be necessary to protect hedges with an electric wire fence.

Internal gates are most satisfactory if they open in both directions. When moving the sheep from one paddock into another the gate can be swung away from them so that the flock can rush out without any getting stuck behind the gate; alternatively one can open the gate in the other direction into the field and against the sheep, so that one can squeeze through without any sheep escaping.

Water
Sheep must have access to water at all times. The most satisfactory source is a mains supply to a trough, fitted with a ball valve. Another possibility is a mains tap in a central position, fitted with a hose leading to the troughs. This presents problems in freezing weather. Where no mains supply is available a water tank can be placed in a small trailer and taken out to the sheep.

Sheep behaviour and handling
The commercial sheep farmer needs dogs to help him move large numbers of sheep away from the mountains or fields that they regard as 'home'. This form of control is unnecessary for the small flock keeper if he studies the natural behaviour of his sheep and bribes them with a few nuts. When sheep are fed from time to time in the area in which they are handled the rattling of a bucket or a familiar call will bring them running in. Movements when handling the flock should be slow and quiet. Sheep are very nervous and if approached too closely become frightened and rush madly away, or, if they cannot do this, will turn to rush past the shepherd. The ideal is to walk slowly and quietly behind the animals so that they move away but do not flee. A gentle 'ssh - ssh' can be used to encourage them on their way. Never shout or wave as they find this threatening, will stop moving and turn to look at you. A stick is useful but only as a barrier to discourage them from running back the way they have come. The new sheep keeper will find it interesting to observe how close he can get to his animals without causing disturbance, and will soon notice that their behaviour is less trusting if a stranger is present. At lambing time the ewes are not disturbed when one sits close to them on a bale or milk crate but they do not like someone standing above them. They lose their timidity when they have new-born lambs to protect and stand before their precious off-spring stamping their feet at any real or imagined threat.

Handling systems
On most sheep farms, close to the buildings, are collections of pens constructed from metal or wooden hurdles. These are known as *handling pens*. When the sheep are brought in from the fields or down from the mountains they are driven

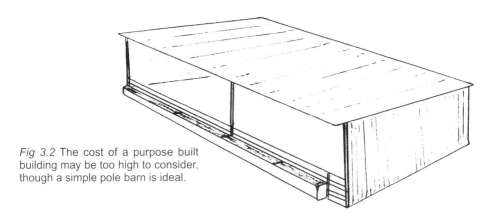

Fig 3.2 The cost of a purpose built building may be too high to consider, though a simple pole barn is ideal.

into the larger pens, and then progressively into smaller ones, which lead to a narrow corridor, known as a *race*. This is used to restrain them while they receive injections or are wormed. When the sheep's feet are being treated the race contains a handling crate, which turns the sheep over so that the feet can be clipped, and a footbath containing medicated fluid. A dip and a shearing area are usually attached to the system.

A small flock requires a much simplified copy of the layout described above *(Fig. 3.1)*. Recent *Groundwater Regulations* have made dipping a very expensive method of controlling parasites, so smallholders are well advised to contact a contractor with a sheep shower to treat serious conditions, and control blowfly themselves by spraying *pour-on* medication on the wool. The essential components of the handling system can be constructed from metal hurdles designed to fit together. These come in 6ft. and 4ft. lengths, and are between 34 and 38 inches high. The higher hurdles need to be strong enough not to bend when supporting the weight of a person, so need to be tried out before purchase. It may be possible to step over the lower hurdles, which is very useful, but these are too low to restrain some of the more energetic breeds. At least six 6 ft. hurdles will be needed; three to form the immovable sides of the pen, two to act as entrance gates and as the fourth side when they are closed, and one to separate off any sheep needing treatment. In addition to the 6ft. hurdles it is useful to have two 4 ft. hurdles to make the ends of a small pen for an individual sheep or lamb. Indeed it is advisable to have as many hurdles as one can afford since there is always a demand for them: individual pens may be needed for sick animals, and for ewes with newborn lambs. (Note that 1 ft. is equivalent to 30 cm).

Ideally the handling system should be set up in a building or yard as a hard floor is needed, and also walls or other structures to support the side hurdles. The alternative is to support them by hurdles placed at right angles.

Movement through the pens should be made easy for the sheep and should lead towards a gate that they can see through, as this will encourage them to move in the desired direction. Catching sheep is best avoided since it is stressful for all parties. When sheep are penned very tightly their movement is so restricted that they can be dosed and injected without problems. A handling crate is useful when clipping feet but is not necessary. A sheep can be held on its rump in a sitting position while the shepherd leans over it to clip the feet. When two people are working together, one can sit on a bale with the sheep sitting between his legs, while the other does the clipping. An alternative for a small flock, and for very large breeds and rams, is to lift up the feet as farriers do when shoeing horses. The sheep can be restrained by putting a collar on it and looping another collar through this and attaching it to the middle bar of a hurdle. When necessary a strap may be fastened to the hurdle and around the body. Sheep become accustomed to this method when it is used regularly.

Outdoor handling pens are best placed in a dry place near the top of the field, as the instinct of fearful sheep is to move uphill to obtain a better view of any threat. As they dislike going into an area where they cannot see a free way ahead, they should run through a gate to a pen concealed on the other side, or they should be fed in the handling area from time to time to get them accustomed to it. The pen can be made more stable by placing it in a corner and attaching it to the fence.

Sheep which must be restricted to a pen due to injury or illness require a water bucket and some hay, which can be pushed behind the hurdle, so that it is not trampled upon. In the field straw bales can be used around the pen to provide extra protection but must be covered by wire netting to prevent the sheep eating them. In bad weather a roof can be constructed out of a sheet of corrugated iron with a bale on top to hold it down.

Housing

In spite of the fact that most British sheep never see the inside of a building, a new sheep farmer possessing a *pole barn (Fig. 3.2)*, a well ventilated shed or polytunnel, should consider housing his sheep at lambing and preferably for eight weeks before. Sheep that are protected from the weather, and have feeding and lambing supervised, suffer fewer ewe losses, and far fewer lamb losses. Some extra hay is required and some straw for bedding, but this is off-set by improved spring grazing. The sheep must be protected from draughts at ground level but good ventilation in the area above is important as sheep are prone to respiratory infections which may accumulate in stale air. The floor of the building can be of bedded earth, and, to avoid foot infections, should have a slight gradient to ensure good drainage. 1.5 sq.m floor space is required per ewe, with not more than thirty ewes penned together. Trough space of 450-500 mm per ewe is needed to avoid bullying, but a frontage of 150mm. per ewe is sufficient for hay. The pole barn in *Fig. 3.2* has a combined feed trough and hay rack forming the front of the building. This is known as a *feed barrier* and has the advantage that it can be filled from outside. Alternatively, nuts can be scattered over the straw after clean bedding has been put down. This avoids the provision of troughs, gives the sheep exercise and occupation, and allows shy feeders to get their share. The sheep must have easy access to water, and an electricity supply is valuable, not only to provide light for the shepherd but also to enable the use of a heat lamp for feeble lambs. Housing improves the lot of the shepherd, encouraging him to spend more time with the flock, leading to a more successful lambing.

Sheep keepers can also make use of a *sheltered yard*, where lambing pens can be erected and the sheep housed, at least at night. If the evening feed is given in the yard the sheep will enter it readily. A lean-to roof constructed along one wall will protect the lambing pens from rain, and the shepherd has the advantage of being within easy reach of the house, and being able to make use of electric power and light.

Equipment

A good assortment of plastic buckets are required and metal or plastic feed troughs are useful but not absolutely necessary. Good foot shears with a serrated edge are a must. Shepherds with small hands can use foot shears designed for lamb's feet. Another necessity is a dosing gun to administer wormer. Where the sheep are to be sprayed with *Vetrazine* or a similar product to protect them from blowflies, the gun used for spraying can also be used for dosing, if cleaned carefully.

Small shears, known as dagging shears, are used for cutting away dirty wool from the sheep's rear end. Needles and disposable syringes are required to give vaccinations, and a spray-on colour marker is useful, otherwise one may treat one sheep twice and one not at all. At lambing ear tags and an applicator are needed, as are rubber castration rings and the instrument for applying them which is known as an *elastrator.* Further small items are listed in *Chapter 8.*

Finally an anti-bacterial spray for the treatment of superficial wounds, fly strike, cuts and abrasions should be in the medicine cupboard, along with a purple medicated spray for the treatment of foot infections. Both are available from farm supplies.

Fig. 3.3 Good foot shears are a must.
Photo: Katie Thear

25

Part 2 Caring for Sheep

Chapter 4 Husbandry Tasks

Checking the sheep or 'lookering'

Ideally this is a daily task, carried out in order to identify problems at an early stage when treatment is more effective and infections have not spread. If the flock is kept away from the holding, or on extensive grazing, they should be seen as often as possible. Looking over the gate every day is not sufficient. Whenever possible take time to walk among the sheep. Not only are problems more easily observed but the sheep become accustomed to the presence of the owner and will be quieter when handled.

Gathering the flock

At certain times (see calendar at the end of this chapter), the sheep should brought into an enclosed area and inspected individually. Their feet should be checked for injuries and infections; their udders for lumps, indicating damage from mastitis; and their mouths for missing front teeth or lumps on the jaws, which may be caused by infections of back teeth. Sheep should have their condition assessed whenever they are handled. This is known as *condition scoring*.

Condition scoring

Many of the conditions from which sheep suffer hinder their grazing or impair their digestion, resulting in rapid weight loss. Only in the month or so following shearing is it possible to tell if a sheep is too fat, too thin or in good condition merely by looking at it. Condition scoring is a method of assessing the condition of a sheep by placing the hand over the backbone in the area just behind the rib cage. You can find this place on yourself, by resting your hands on your hips, with the thumbs pointing forwards, and the fingers touching each other over the spine. In sheep the bones of the spine are more prominent than in man, and feel sharp if the animal has little muscle and very little fat (score 2), *(Fig. 4.1)*. An over-fat sheep has such a thick fat layer that it is difficult to feel the bones of the spine (score 4). A sheep in good condition has a full muscle (assessed by feeling the area on either side of the spine), and only a moderate fat layer, allowing the spine to feel smooth and rounded (score 3 - 3.5). Sheep are not very co-operative models when condition scoring is being practised. Since dogs are used to being

Fig. 4.1 Body Condition Scoring

This system is only for assessing the physical condition of sheep, to correct nutrition or health status. It is unsuitable for grading lambs for slaughter, where further factors have to be taken into account. In body condition scoring the classes run from 0 - emaciated, where the animal is only skin and bone and near to death, to 5 - very fat, where neither the vertical bones of the spine nor the horizontal ones can be felt through the fat cover. Sheep should never be allowed to reach this condition because this amount of fat is injurious to health. Treatment is a diet of either poor hay or straw and water.

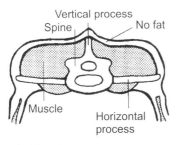

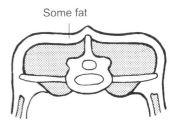

Score 1 - Very lean
The spine is prominent and sharp, the horizontal processes feel sharp and one can easily push one's fingers under them. The muscle which runs between the spine and the horizontal processes feels thin. There is no fat cover. When a sheep is as lean as this the cause must be determined and action taken to improve the condition.

Score 2 - Lean
The spine feels prominent but smooth, with the vertical processes detectable as corrugations rather than sharp points. The horizontal processes are smooth and rounded, but one can still push one's fingers underneath them. The muscle is of moderate depth with a thin covering of fat. Sheep should be in better condition than this at most times of the year.

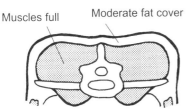

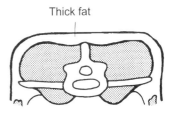

Score 3 - Good condition
The vertical processes are smooth and rounded, and one can only feel the bones by pressing. The horizontal processes are also smooth and rounded, and one needs to press hard to find the ends. The muscle is full and the fat cover moderate.

Score 4 - Fat
When pressed the spine is felt only as a hard line. The horizontal processes cannot be felt. The muscle is full and has a thick covering of fat. This is too fat, except for Lowland rams at the beginning of tupping.

stroked and patted, it is useful to score some dogs before starting on sheep. The importance of condition scoring cannot be over-emphasised, and should be done as a matter of course whenever the sheep are being handled.

The most important times to condition score are noted in the husbandry calendar below. Mountain sheep score 0.5 less than Lowland sheep, and Primitive breeds also score less because they store fat around the internal organs rather than under the skin. In early pregnancy sheep cannot be scored because it is unwise to handle them. Considerable time must be allowed to improve low condition scores. To achieve C.S. 3.5 a ewe under score 2.0 needs 6-8 weeks, while 4-6 weeks are necessary for a ewe scoring 2-3. Only 2-4 weeks are needed to reach 3.5 from 3.0.

Sheep's teeth

Without sound teeth a sheep cannot graze effectively, it will lose condition and eventually die. Therefore teeth inspections are important when buying sheep and checking older animals.

Sheep have a bony pad in the front of the upper jaw against which the eight incisors in the lower jaw bite. Molars are present in both the upper and lower jaw. Inspect these teeth by feeling the outside of the jaw to determine if there are lumps or sharp edges which could indicate problems.

Lambs acquire eight incisors soon after birth. At about 15 months the central pair are replaced by larger adult teeth, and the sheep is known as a *two-tooth*. The adult teeth appear at yearly intervals, the animal being progressively known as a *four-tooth* and a *six-tooth*. When the sheep is somewhat over four years of age the sheep has eight incisors and is known as *full-mouthed*. When older sheep start to lose their teeth they become *broken-mouthed* and may have to be culled.

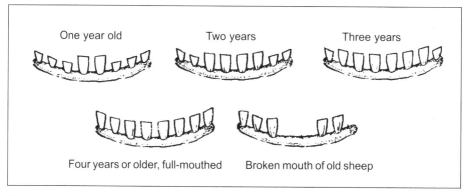

Fig. 4.2 Establishing the approximate age of sheep by examining the teeth

A Typical Husbandry Calendar

It is useful to draw up a calendar showing the times when husbandry tasks, and alterations to the feeding regime, etc, should be carried out. The following calendar is for a flock lambing in mid-March, and can be adjusted to suit your own lambing date. Care of the previous year's lambs is not included, as this varies considerably from flock to flock.

July
Wean the lambs. Check and score the ewes. After inspection of feet, udders and teeth, identify sheep to be culled. Increase feed for thin ewes.

September
Check and score rams and ewes. Adjust feed to achieve condition score 3.5 (3.0 for hill sheep) by tupping. Worm if weather warm and wet.

End September
Increase feed if necessary. Worm and score rams and ewes, and check feet. Crutch, ie, clip wool from around the tail, if the wool is dirty or likely to impede the ram.

20 October
Turn rams in with ewes. Raddled rams require colour change on 4 and 20 November. *Raddle* is colour which is applied to the lower chest of the ram to mark the ewes as he covers them.

Beginning January (or at housing)
Worm and condition score ewes, treat feet. Separate out thin ewes, and old ewes and young ewes for special feeding. Check rams this month but do not worm.

1 February
At 6 weeks pre-lambing start to increase feed, two weeks earlier if straw or flat rate fed.

8 February
From 6 - 2 weeks pre-lambing, inject ewes and rams with booster vaccine to protect against clostridial diseases and pasteurellosis. The date will depend on the brand.

End February
Check lambing supplies. Erect lambing pens and check fencing (young lambs can get through very small gaps).

Mid-March
First lambs born from 10 March, majority from 15 March. Dress lambs' navels at birth, castrate and dock tails at 24 hours for singles, 48 hours for smaller lambs and multiple births, within the first week for very small or sickly lambs. Apply ear tags or other identification at the same time.

March/April
Feed ewes with concentrate for six weeks following lambing. This should contain magnesium if there is a danger of grass staggers (magnesium deficiency).

May
Worm ewes at three and six weeks post lambing, if the ewes and lambs are put onto grazing which has been used the previous year. Worm lambs at six weeks and then three weekly until the worm threat has subsided. Creep feed lambs if the grazing is limited. Score all sheep when worming.

May/June
Shear the ewes. Protect lambs against blowfly by dipping or spraying, and do the same for the ewes following re-growth of the wool after shearing. Vaccinate the lambs at 10 - 12 weeks post lambing, and give the booster vaccination 4 - 6 weeks later.

Chapter 5 Common Infections and Parasites

Although sheep are subject to a large number of infections and parasites, the most common can be prevented by vaccination or kept under control by the methods described in this chapter. Some sheep infections can be transmitted to humans so sheep handlers should protect themselves by wearing plastic disposable gloves when handling sick sheep, lambing ewes and new-born lambs, and also when administering *Orf* vaccine.

Pregnant women and young children are especially susceptible to some sheep diseases, and should never have contact with lambing ewes, and new-born or scouring lambs (lambs with diarrhoea).

Foot care

Foot infections are a common problem in sheep and can have serious consequences. A sheep with painful feet cannot graze efficiently and soon loses condition, moreover foot infections can give rise to attack by blowflies to the feet and the skin. New-born lambs may be infected through the navel by bacteria present in the feet of the mother, and when the back feet of rams are affected they may be unable to mount the ewes. Sheep that are limping, standing with a foot raised, grazing on their knees *(Fig. 5.1)* or grazing while lying down, should have their feet inspected and treated at the earliest opportunity.

The sheep's hoof consists of two parts called the *cleats*, *digits* or *claws*. The claws are made of a very hard outer-casing of horn, called the *hoof wall*, which protects an inner, softer area. The hoof wall grows more quickly than the rest of the hoof to allow for wear from rough ground and may get so long that it bends inwards underneath the foot, allowing bits of grit to be trapped and injure the softer sole.Alternatively, the hoof wall may turn outwards, and pieces of grit may cause the lower part of the wall to be forced away from the rest of the foot.

Since injuries to the feet allow bacteria to enter, the hoof wall should be trimmed with foot shears from time to time, so that there is only sufficient horn protruding above the hoof to bear the weight of the sheep. When the hoof wall has separated from the hoof, the separated part is trimmed away from the rest of the hoof. Care must be taken to avoid bleeding, and wounds to the foot treated immediately with an anti-bacterial spray.

Sometimes the sole of the hoof is infected by bacteria which cause layers of horn to separate, enabling bacteria to multiply in the pockets. This condition is known as *Foot rot.* The layers are pared away with care and the hoof treated. When the hoof is badly affected it is best to separate the sheep from the flock,

Fig 5.1 This ewe is grazing on her knees and should have her feet examined.
Photo: Laura Densmore

keep it in a small paddock or pen, and carry out the treatment over a few days. If the animal is kept in a building the floor should be disinfected. When more than one hoof is infected, grazing will be impeded, both by the condition and by the cure, so it is best to treat one hoof at a time. Since the bacterium causing foot rot cannot live outside the foot for more than ten days it is advisable to move freshly treated sheep to new pasture and not return them for twelve days.

Foot infections are very contagious, therefore new stock should be quarantined and treated. In wet, warm weather (over 10^0C), conditions are ideal for the spread of the disease. In a small flock constant attention to the condition of the feet is important, since the grazing area is likely to be restricted and infection can pass easily from one sheep to another. In a very small flock regular foot inspections and the use of an anti-bacterial spray may be sufficient to control the disease, and when a bad case is found, a footbath solution containing *Zinc sulphate* may be made up in a bucket, and the sheep induced to put her foot in it for three to five minutes. Many owners feel that the purchase of a footbath is worthwhile. It is important that the sheep stand in the solution for at least the recommended period, and that their feet are reasonably clean before treatment. Footbaths which are long and narrow are designed to fit into a handling race. Rectangular footbaths, made to fit into a pen, are less common, but have the advantage that sheep stand in them more willingly, and for a very small flock a plastic footbath for two sheep is available.

Internal parasite control

Stomach and intestinal worms

Unfortunately sheep are subject to parasitic worms which invade the stomach and gut. On large holdings it is possible to move the sheep every year to fields that have been ploughed, cut for hay or used for cattle in the previous year, and are therefore almost worm free. This management system is not possible for the average smallholder, who will have to cope with the problem by carrying out a worming programme. The worming programme, described under 'May' in the calendar in *Chapter 4*, is suitable. If hay is made on the holding the re-growth of grass, known as the aftermath, will be worm free, and it can be used for lambs to graze after weaning.

Adult sheep, with the exception of ewes after lambing, are largely immune to round worms, but lambs are highly susceptible. The larvae damage the lining of the stomach and gut, resulting in diarrhoea and weight loss.

Worm eggs are destroyed if the weather is too cold or too dry and hot, and young larvae are destroyed if they are eaten by adult sheep. Worming the ewes in the six weeks following lambing removes a high proportion of worms from the pasture, greatly improving it for the lambs. The threat from worms is at its greatest in warm, damp weather (temperature of 10^0C). This explains the large outbreaks which can happen in a damp July or August, when eggs dropped over many weeks hatch together.

Many worming preparations (called *anthelmintics*) are available. They belong to three groups. Immunity to the preparation can build up, so each year one should change to a wormer of a different group. Your supplier will give you advice on this. Sheep are wormed while standing in a pen or race, preferably with several packed tightly together so that movement is difficult. One hand is placed beneath the sheep's chin, while the other hand operates the dosing gun, which is put into the back corner of the mouth, through the gap between the front and back teeth, and over the back part of the tongue. The trigger should be pressed steadily so that the sheep can swallow easily. This avoids the wormer trickling out of the mouth, or entering the windpipe and lungs. It is important to give the correct dosage for the weight of the animal. When a group of lambs is to be dosed, the heaviest is weighed, and the remainder of the group given the dose appropriate for the heaviest. The same applies to groups of ewes. The worming regime given in the husbandry calendar is very effective on restricted grazing. By worming the ewes at three and six weeks post lambing they will clear the pasture of worms before the lambs start grazing seriously.

Lungworms live in the main airways and lungs of young sheep causing inflammation, coughing and occasionally pneumonia. The main attacks are in late summer and autumn. The wormers described in the preceding paragraph are also used for lung worms.

Many parasites tend to be local, for instance **Liver fluke** is a serious parasite in some boggy areas, so information about possible problems should be sought from your neighbours and vet.

External parasites

Blowfly strike

This is usually caused by the greenbottle fly and occasionally by other flies. They lay their eggs in wounds or on the soiled parts of sheep. After a few days the eggs hatch into maggots which feed on the flesh of the sheep causing intense distress. The sheep try to rub or nibble the affected areas. They lose condition rapidly, and the open wounds leave them subject to secondary infections. Mild cases heal quickly if the wool is clipped away and the affected area treated with an insecticidal cream. Antiseptic or disinfectant cannot be used as they are too toxic, and inhibit the healing process. In serious cases the vet should be consulted, and it may be necessary to have the animal destroyed.

Prevention of strike is very important. Sheep can be dipped, or sprayed with a pour-on, between May and September. Both these methods are successful for varying periods and may need to be used once, twice, or sometimes three times. Sheep can have wool around the tail shortened (*crutched*), and soiled wool is always removed. Head wounds on fighting rams, and wounds arising at shearing, are treated with a suitable fly repellent.

Scouring sheep should be treated immediately as should sheep with foot rot because the smell is attractive to flies, and the area between the claws of the hoof an ideal site to lay eggs. When an affected sheep lies down, the wool next to the foot can become soiled and maggots enter the fleece. Since flies enjoy the shade of trees it is best to keep sheep away when there are a lot of flies about.

There are many other external parasites affecting sheep but as many are uncommon and some local, information from your neighbours and vet is important.

Vaccinations

Vaccinations act by stimulating the immune response of the body to a disease. Following vaccination the immune system produces antibodies when it comes in contact with the infection. It is standard practice to vaccinate sheep annually against a range of infections caused by the clostridia group of bacteria and known as *Clostridial diseases*. This injection is often combined with protection to *Pasteurella* (pneumonia). Your vet may also advise vaccination if your flock is subject to severe attacks of some other diseases, such as Orf (see following section).

Antibodies are transmitted to human babies through their mother's blood supply. This is not the case with lambs. They receive antibodies after birth from the ewe's colostrum, and are at risk of infection if they do not drink a sufficient quantity in about the first four hours of life. Orphan lambs should receive colostrum from another ewe, or, failing this, an artificial preparation containing antibodies. To ensure that lambing ewes are producing a high level of antibodies to clostridial diseases and pasteurella, they are vaccinated 4-6 weeks before lambing, which covers them for a year and their lambs for at least ten weeks.

Vaccination packs contain detailed instructions which should be read carefully as the various brands have differing application times. Vaccines are injected beneath the skin in a place where the wool is clean and dry. The mid-neck region is often chosen as a suitable site. Vaccination of lambs is described in *Chapter 9.*

Common infections also affecting humans (Zoonoses)

Orf is a viral infection which causes small blisters around the muzzle, usually in the late summer or autumn. When the blisters break secondary infections can enter so it may be wise to spray them with an anti-bacterial spray. Plastic disposable gloves must be worn as orf can lead to serious illness in humans. A more virulent form of orf can attack ewes and their young lambs. The advice of your vet must be sought at once and he may recommend vaccination.

Abortions may be caused by several agents some of which severely affect pregnant women! In case the cause is infectious the ewe must be separated at once, and if a second case occurs the vet contacted, as some infections causing abortion spread rapidly.

Scouring, i.e. diarrhoea. In adult sheep this is usually caused by worms or digestive problems. Worming and a diet of hay normally return a sheep to good health. This is not the case with young lambs, as they are subject to gut infections. The vet should be consulted as lambs decline rapidly due to the resulting dehydration. Some infections causing scouring in lambs can be transmitted to young children so they should be kept well away from infected lambs.

Diseases causing irritation

It is best to consult your vet whenever you observe a sheep constantly rubbing itself (unless this is caused by blowfly) as this might indicate one of two very serious illnesses - **Scrapie**, which is caused by an agent similar to that causing BSE, and **Sheep scab**. It is a criminal offence to fail to treat sheep visibly affected with sheep scab and all other sheep in the flock. *(See Chapter 12).*

Fig. 5.2 Clun Forest ewes. Note the ear tags for identification. *Photo: Katie Thear*

Ovine conjunctivitis

Inflammation of the eye is quite common and is often caused when hay seeds etc. scratch the eye ball and admit infection. Affected sheep should be isolated immediately as the infection spreads rapidly. Your vet will prescribe an ointment which is usually very effective.

Mastitis

This is infection of the udder. When a lactating sheep is seen to walk stiffly, is preventing her lambs from sucking or has a lamb that is standing with a hunched back which indicates hunger, she must be penned at once. If the udder feels hot and hard the vet must be contacted and is likely to prescribe an antibiotic. The lambs will have to be removed and young lambs bottle fed.

Mastitis leads to the death of many ewes and others have to be culled at weaning because the udder has been damaged by the infection.

Poisonous plants

Sheep must be kept away from garden plants as many of these are poisonous. Yew, lily of the valley, lupins, deadly nightshade and woody nightshade may occur in hedges and are toxic. Bracken in quantity is poisonous as is ragwort, the latter being especially dangerous when wilted or dry in hay. Green acorns are toxic. If sheep are seen eating them they should be moved to another pasture.

Medical records

Sheep-keepers are obliged to keep medical records *(See Government Regulations, Reference section)* and are not permitted to send animals for slaughter for a specific time following worming or other medication. This is known as the *Withdrawal period* and is printed on the leaflet enclosed with the preparation.

Chapter 6   Feeding Sheep

The digestive system of sheep

Humans cannot digest grass because the main constituent, *cellulose*, is too tough. Adult sheep have overcome this obstacle by chewing very thoroughly, a process known as *cudding*, and making *use of bacteria* to break down the vegetable matter for them, as a gardener does with his compost heap.

Cudding

Grazing sheep are out in the open and can be seen by predators, so they hasten the process by swallowing the grass without chewing it. Cudding takes place for about eight hours in twenty four, mainly at night, and while the sheep is lying in a protected place. When cudding a small portion of feed is brought up into the mouth; the liquid is pressed out and swallowed; the cud is chewed fifty to sixty times for about a minute and then swallowed again. After five seconds pause the procedure is repeated. For this system to work satisfactorily the sheep needs to produce large quantities of saliva and have good teeth.

The digestive tract

This looks complicated *(See Fig. 6.1)*, because there appear to be four stomachs of varying size. In fact only the last of these, the *abomasum*, is the *true stomach* in which food is digested by *enzymes,* as it is in a human. The first chamber, the *rumen*, is very large and contains the bacteria. The second is the *reticulum* which contains liquid to moisten the cud, the third, the *omasum*, removes the liquid to be re-used in saliva. Food remains pass from the abomasum through the intestine to be secreted as pellets. Loose stools may indicate very lush grazing or a digestive problem.

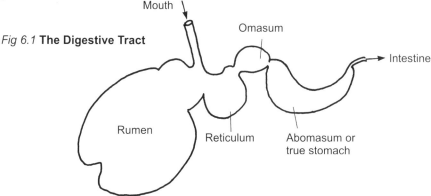

Fig 6.1 **The Digestive Tract**

The bacteria break down the vegetable matter into *fatty acids*, *methane* and *heat*. The heat warms the sheep; the fatty acids are absorbed into the sheep's blood stream and provide it with energy; only the methane goes to waste. This is burped up silently through the sheep's nose to avoid attracting the attention of predators. Large numbers of bacteria pass from the rumen into the true stomach where they are digested, providing the sheep with *protein*.

For most of the year a sheep lives on grass alone and receives sufficient nutrition to rear one lamb. Most farmers, however, hope that their sheep will produce a high proportion of large twins. To achieve this the sheep requires extra feed, and, as the space in the abdomen is restricted by the size of the lambs, cereal with added protein is usually given as a space-saving supplement to hay in the last weeks of pregnancy. The bacteria that break down the starch in cereal are not the same as those that break down hay and operate at different levels of acidity, so the introduction of the new feed must be very slow, ideally 2-3 weeks, to allow the sheep to build up more of these bacteria. A careful balance must be kept so that the higher acid levels caused by feeding cereal do not impair the digestion of hay and inflame the rumen, a condition that can lead to death.

The bacteria which break down protein continue to do so after they have satisfied their own needs, resulting in an excess production of ammonia which may depress the ewe's appetite. For this reason pelleted feeds contain some proteins which cannot be broken down by bacteria and pass unaltered out of the rumen to be digested in the abomasum. The feeds and feeding regimes described at the end of this chapter are designed to avoid nutritional problems during the pre-lambing period.

The digestive system of lambs differs from that of adult sheep because at birth the rumen is very small and has no bacterial population. Lambs start to acquire bacteria by chewing on little bits of hay and straw. When a lamb runs to the ewe to drink, or sees its bottle arriving, the entrance to the rumen closes, allowing the milk to pass directly into the true stomach, which is already fully developed. By eight weeks of age the rumen is fully grown, but, as the ewe is producing very little milk from six weeks after birth, the lambs experience a two week period when their nutrition level declines somewhat. This problem period is addressed in the feeding regimes described later in this chapter.

Sheep feeds for a small flock

Grass

This consists not only of *cellulose*, but also of *lignin*, which is even tougher. It gives the plant its stiffness, is found mainly in the stalks, and is hard for sheep to digest. Hence coarse grass is less nutritious than the soft, young grass of spring which can support both ewes and lambs.

The sugars in grass decline by late July, growth ceases, and the nutritive value also declines.

In the autumn the grass starts to grow again, and, though less nutritious than the spring grass, provides a valuable feed for the ewes when they are being mated. In winter grass growth ceases, the quality is low, and after Christmas, or even earlier, the sheep may need hay.

From January onwards sheep can damage the grass buds of the coming year by treading on the plants. On a limited acreage this is an important consideration and may lead flock owners to house their sheep during the eight weeks before lambing.

Hay

Hay can be made or bought. Hay making on a small acreage is problematic as the cost of a tractor and the necessary equipment is rarely justified, and contractors are unwilling to come at a busy time for a small return.

When buying hay for the first time it is wise to take an experienced companion because hay quality is very variable. Good quality hay is leafy, has a fresh colour and a scent of summer. When the weather has delayed hay making, or the pasture has been grazed too late in the spring, the hay can be very coarse.

Good quality hay from the previous year is sometimes for sale; it will have lost the fresh colour and scent, but if it is leafy, it can be very useful. Hay that has started to go mouldy is useless, as it affects the health of the sheep.

Hay bales come in three sizes: *small and rectangular*; *large and rectangular*; and *round*. The rectangular bales are constructed like loaves of cut bread, with the hay coming away in convenient slices. Small bales weigh about 20kg. and are easy to handle. Large bales must be stacked with the use of a tractor. They have hay slices which are large and cumbersome, making them difficult to handle when hay racks are being filled in the field, but they are not too much of a problem if the sheep are fed in the building in which the bales are stacked. Round bales are constructed like huge Swiss rolls. They require special handling equipment and are unsuitable for the small flock owner.

Hay can be fed in the field in *hay racks* or *hay boxes*. The hay racks must be low so that seeds do not get into the sheep's eyes, and racks have the advantage that they can be moved around to avoid the field getting muddied. The boxes waste less hay because the sheep feed with their heads inside them, but they require a hard standing as they are difficult to move.

Hay boxes sited endways on to a fence and fitted with a moveable lid, can be filled from outside the field *(Fig.6.2)*. They can be used for feeding nuts if all the sheep in the field have space to feed at the box together.

Fig 6.2 This haybox and feed block container has a removeable lid for filling. The sheep feed from both sides. *Photo: Mary Castell*

Straw

Straw should look bright and have a fresh, golden colour. It is used as bedding for housed sheep. When the straw is placed on the floor in heaps, the sheep eat the leafy bits and spread the rest around the building. Barley straw can be used to feed housed sheep as long as they are given fresh straw after they have eaten 60% - 70% of their daily ration. The nutritive value of straw is low, and needs supplementing with cereal. In arable areas the cost of straw and a cereal supplement may compare favourably with the price of hay. Straw is packed in the same type of bales as hay, and the same disadvantages apply to the large bales.

Pelleted feeds

Pelleted feeds are used to supplement forage at *tupping* (mating), during the winter months and over the lambing period.

Sugar beet pellets are useful at tupping and during the winter because they can be scattered on the grass and provide the sheep with energy.

Cereal based pellets are known as *concentrates*. They contain some minerals and vitamins as well as the extra protein necessary for a lambing or lactating ewe. Feed specifications on the bag give a percentage of CP; this is *crude protein*, the term for the total protein. Part of this is *RDP* (rumen degradable protein), and part *UDP* (undegradable dietary protein). The latter is the protein that is not broken down in the rumen and is important for the lambing ewe. The total protein content varies between 14% and 18%. 14% is sufficient except during lambing when 16% or 18% protein is required.

Feed blocks and molasses based liquid feeds are used when the sheep cannot be fed daily or when it is unwise to disturb them. Liquid feed, provided through a ball feeder *(Fig. 6.3)* is not as hard on the teeth and is preferable for older sheep.

Feeding regimes

Feeding regimes are very variable and adapted to a wide range of environments, and requirements of the market.

Mountain and upland sheep only receive hay in very severe weather and are fed little or no cereal at lambing, but they are not expected to produce twins or heavy meat lambs. On intensive lowland farms, where the ewe produces large, fast-growing twin lambs, she may require extra feed at mating; she will certainly need hay in the winter, also supplementary feeding for six weeks before lambing and the first six weeks of lactation. The small amounts of supplementary feed given at tupping and during the winter do not cause digestive problems.

Feeding during the tupping period
(the six weeks following the introduction of the ram).
During this time the main consideration is that the feed should be sufficient to keep the ewes at condition score 3.0-3.5 (2.5 for hill ewes) without inducing stress which can be caused by pushing to get to the feed. A self-help system such as feed blocks or liquid feed is a good solution. Sugar beet nuts can be scattered on the pasture but not cereal based nuts as they disintegrate. Small flock owners may have a yard or building in which the ewes are accustomed to be handled and fed. When this contains sufficient trough space to prevent jostling it is a good place to feed the ewes, and if raddle (colouring matter put on the ram's chest to identify the ewes covered) is used, it will be easy to note down the tag numbers of ewes that have been tupped. 0.25-0.5kg. daily of concentrate per ewe should be sufficient for medium sized ewes during this period.

Feeding during mid-pregnancy
Feeding should continue to maintain the condition score at the same level, or only a couple of points under, because the development of the placenta is taking place and any check in its growth will lead to undersized lambs in spite of good feeding in late pregnancy. From the second half of December the grazing will need supplementing with hay, fed ad lib. Consumption will be about 1kg. daily for a medium sized ewe.

Fig 6.3 A ewe feeding from a ball feeder. *Photo: Dallas Keith Ltd.*

Feeding during the last six weeks of pregnancy

During the final two months of pregnancy the lambs complete an astonishing 85% of their growth and naturally the feeding of the ewes has to reflect the high demands placed on them. This is especially important in the final two weeks when the expanded uterus pushes up against the rumen, thereby diminishing its volume and restricting the intake of bulky feeds such as hay. The feeding rates given are for a 70 kg ewe lambing in March and can be adjusted for sheep of varying weights. It is important that all the ewes receive sufficient feed; therefore it is necessary to provide adequate trough frontage, 450 mm per ewe, and space at the hay rack, 150 mm per ewe. Horned ewes require rather more space.

Stepped-rate feeding

The pre-lambing period is divided into six weeks. In weeks 6 and 5, 0.5kg of concentrate is given daily; in weeks 4 and 3, 0.75kg; and in the final 2 weeks, 0.90kg, which is divided into two feeds, one in the morning and one in the evening. The object of dividing the feed in two is to avoid a very high acid level in the rumen. There will be some impairment of forage digestion after each feed, but only for 2-3 hours. A cautious owner may prefer to give the sheep 0.25kg. for a week before serious feeding begins, and may decide to accustom the animals to twice daily feeding by starting this in weeks 4 or 3.

Flat-rate feeding

The same quantity of feed is given, but divided equally over the six weeks, with an additional introductory week in which the feed is built up gradually. This system avoids the risks involved in giving very high rates of feed in the final two weeks, but means that the ewe will have to rely on the resources she has built up over the entire period. Splitting the feeds into two is not so important but is advisable in the final two weeks. This system is useful for owners who do not raddle or scan their sheep, and are unable to adjust feeding to an expected lambing date.

Feeding ewes after lambing

Sheep milk is highly nutritious and its production places great demands on the ewe. *Feeding should continue as in stepped-rate feeding, but in the reverse order.* A ewe that has just produced twins can be expected to lose 0.5 condition score, and another 0.5 or more is lost during lactation, even when feeding is continued at the suggested rate. When a lamb is three or four weeks old it is taking the highest quantity of milk; by six weeks it is receiving a considerable amount of nutrition from grass, and the feeding of the ewe is no longer necessary. Digestive problems in the ewe are unlikely at this time because the rumen returns to a normal size after lambing.

Feeding lambs (for bottle fed lambs see chapter 10)

Some lambs can be sold to the butcher at about 16 weeks of age, and may need creep feeding from three weeks to improve their nutrition until after the rumen is fully developed at eight weeks. Creep feed consists of very small nuts with a high protein content which are fed in a creep feeder with adjustable bars to exclude the ewes, once the lambs have taken to the feed. Beet shreds can also be fed in this way to growing lambs.

Smaller lambs and those from slower growing breeds need more time before they are ready for market. The feeding regime for these lambs will depend on the owner. He may be able to fatten them on the autumn grass or can give them extra

feed to accelerate their growth. Some lambs are kept till after Christmas and fattened when they have grown to a good size. Where grazing is limited in area or quality, it is usually best to sell lambs as *store lambs* before the end of the summer. These are lambs that go to another farmer to fatten.

Fig. 6.4 Lamb creep feeder.
Photo: Ritchie Farm Equipment

42

Part III The Shepherd's Year

Chapter 7 Weaning, Tupping, Early and Mid-Pregnancy

The sheep's breeding season is controlled by a hormone called *melatonin*, which is only produced during the hours of darkness. In humans this is the hormone involved in the control of our sleeping rhythms. Breeding is inhibited during the summer, when nights are short and the production of melatonin low, and sexual activity is induced as melatonin increases during the longer nights of autumn and winter. This has the advantage that the sheep will be in good condition for mating from the autumn flush of grass, and the gestation period of about five months ensures that the lambs will be born when the spring grass is beginning to grow.

The majority of British breeds are sexually most active from October to December. Putting the tup in with the ewes early or late results in fewer multiple births and more barren ewes. Ewes have a gestation period of about five months, 147-151 days in most breeds, less in some. They ovulate for one to two days and come into season every sixteen days. Ewe lambs are more variable. Rams produce some sperm throughout the year but only become sexually active as daylight decreases. They also become more aggressive and must be approached carefully, especially when they are with the ewes.

Preparing the ewes for tupping

Weaning

The date of weaning is the beginning of the preparation for tupping. All ewes lose some condition during pregnancy and lactation, and ewes with twins or triplets may lose a considerable amount. To allow for recovery a minimum of two months must pass between weaning and tupping, in general the longer the better. Weaning usually takes place between 12 and 16 weeks following birth. Although at 12 weeks a lamb is receiving almost all its nutrients from grass, weaning is stressful for the lamb, and may result in little or no weight gain for up to three weeks, therefore weaning may have to be delayed for lambs that are near finishing (almost ready for the butcher). When weaning some stress can be avoided by allowing the lambs to remain in their accustomed surroundings, and removing the ewes to a barn to be dried out on a diet of straw and water. Alternatively the ewes can be transferred to poor grazing at a high stocking rate. A period in the barn is preferable because cases of mastitis are avoided by rapid drying-off. Also the ewes and lambs are less likely to be distressed by hearing each other.

Culling

It is usual to inspect the ewes at this time and cull (reject and sell) those that are unsatisfactory. The main reasons for culling are lumps in the udder; a prolapse at lambing; barrenness for two seasons; and very bad feet. Ewes may also be culled if their teeth are poor, if they are poor milkers, if their behaviour is difficult, or if their condition has so deteriorated due to age or disease that they will not be fit to lamb by the autumn.

Condition scoring

Once the ewes have been dried-off they must be condition scored. Those over 2.5 can be put on good grazing and left to regain condition, while the best grazing must be reserved for underweight ewes. At tupping the ewes should have a condition score between 3.0 and 3.5 (2.5 - 3.0 for hill sheep). Ewes unlikely to achieve this can be fed 0.25kg to 0.5kg of cereal daily for six weeks before and during tupping. Overweight ewes can be put on restricted grazing until they reach a score of 3.0 - 3.5. Ewe lambs can be mated if they have attained two thirds of their adult body-weight by the time the tup is introduced. They must receive sufficient feed during the winter to enable them to continue their growth as well as support the pregnancy.

Flushing

Two or three weeks before the rams are introduced, the ewes are encouraged to shed many eggs by giving them very good grazing, or grazing supplemented by feed blocks. This is known as *flushing* and should be continued throughout tupping. Hill ewes should be flushed only if there will be sufficient good grazing in the spring to support ewes with twins.

Preparing the rams for tupping

Rams should be checked regularly throughout the year, and not forgotten when the ewes are vaccinated, wormed or treated for fly strike. Special attention should be given to their feet before tupping because foot rot can lower their sperm count for up to eight weeks. If this condition is not spotted before the pre-tupping check there may not be sufficient time to effect a cure. At eight weeks pre-tupping the following checks should be made:

Body condition

Tups that are thin should be fed 1lb. of 18% C.P. (crude protein) nuts per day to enable them to reach a condition score of 3.5 - 4.0 by tupping. If they do not improve sufficiently rapidly, increase the ration gradually to up to 2lbs. per day.

Fig 7.1 A ram following a ewe he has just mounted and intends to cover again.
Photo: Mary Castell

Teeth

Inspect the incisors and feel along the outside of the jaw to check that there are no swellings under the molars. A ram with poor teeth may need to be replaced, or be given supplementary feeding.

Feet

Care of the feet is of primary importance. A ram whose response to the ewes is *"My feet are killing me"*, will not be able to work satisfactorily. Clip the feet and medicate if necessary. Observe the ram regularly to make sure that no foot problems develop before the ram is turned in with the ewes.

Worms

If there is any scouring, worm immediately; otherwise wait to worm the rams until a couple of weeks before tupping.

General health

Check that the testicles are even and firm, with no lumps, and observe the rams to see if they are passing water normally. If there are problems contact your vet.

Inspect the eyes for inflammation and if necessary treat for conjunctivitis. Orf may attack the sheath and sometimes the penis, and will make it impossible to use the animal. Check the body and legs for lumps and abrasions.

Some smallholders have flocks which include ewes of several breeds and may wish to use a ram from one breed on the entire flock. They should be aware that there is evidence to show that rams prefer ewes that look like their mothers, or foster mothers, therefore these ewes will be covered first when the ram has a choice of ewes on heat.

Tupping

If the ewes are all to have a chance of being served within the first seventeen days, the number of ewes that a ram is to serve must be limited to 40 (*Fig. 7.1*) or not more than 20 for a ram lamb. Two rams should not be put in together as they will fight each other, fail to concentrate on serving the ewes, and may injure or kill one another. Three rams together tend to ignore one another. When two tups are being used they can be put in separate paddocks, preferably non-adjacent.

The use of raddle

Raddle is the colouring agent put upon the ram's lower chest between his front legs to mark every ewe he covers. In a large flock the colour of the raddle is changed every week or every 17 days to give an approximate indication of the date of lambing of the group of ewes showing the same colour. Ewes that return to service will show two colours 17 days apart. The final colour, often black, is applied after 36 days. When a large number of ewes return to service, the ram may not be very fertile.

The traditional method of preparing raddle is to mix the raddle powder with vegetable oil (I add a little soft margarine), and smear it on the ram. This will have to be repeated every two to three days depending on the ram's level of activity. A more modern method makes use of a harness to which a coloured crayon is fixed. Although the crayon is designed to last seventeen days, during which time all the ewes will have come on heat, the harness must be checked several times during this period to make sure that it has not loosened, or worked down through the wool where it can rub the ram's skin.

The owner of a small flock who is letting the sheep into an enclosed area daily, can be even more accurate in estimating the lambing date by noting down the ear tag number of the ewes that have been covered each day. He can make this job quite simple if he sprays a small spot of colour on the sheep when the number has been noted, so that he will not be inspecting more ears than necessary. An estimated lambing date is a valuable piece of information, not only because it indicates when sheep should be closely watched, and perhaps individually penned, but also because the feeding regime can be more accurate, with considerable savings in feed and fewer over-fat ewes.

Feeding the flock during tupping
Rams must be in very good condition (C.S. 4.0) at the beginning of tupping. Even on good quality grass they lose condition, both from the energy they are expending and the limited time they have to graze. When the grazing is not sufficiently good it is necessary to offer supplementary feeding. *See Chapter 6*, under feeding regimes.

Early pregnancy
This covers the first six to eight weeks after the rams have been introduced, depending on the length of the mating period.

At mating a well nourished ewe will shed several eggs. These will be fertilised when the sperm has moved up the reproductive tract of the ewe. Stress can interfere with this process, resulting in unfertilised eggs. The fertilised eggs, now called *embryos*, pass down the oviduct into the uterus, where they eventually implant in the uterine wall to become *foetuses*. It is thought that about a quarter of embryos are lost in the first month of pregnancy. If they die within the first twelve days the ewe will return to the ram about 17 days after the first mating.

To maintain good condition throughout early pregnancy, it is important to keep to the same diet and level of feeding as has been given before and during mating. Ewes in poor condition, or subject to stress because of handling or a change in the feeding regime, are more likely to lose some, or perhaps all, the embryos. The nutritional value of grass is very variable in the autumn so it may be necessary to fill the hay racks.

Mid-pregnancy
During the middle month of the five months of pregnancy, condition must be maintained in order for the placenta to develop satisfactorily. The end of this month is a good time to do a careful inspection of the ewes. They are condition scored, and any that are old, young (about one year), have missing teeth, or are in poor condition, are separated out for special care. Feet are attended to, and sheep that are to be housed are wormed at housing. Other ewes can be wormed at the same time or at lambing. Excess and dirty wool is usually removed from the rear end of the sheep with dagging shears, to enable lambs to find the udder more easily and the shepherd to observe the progress of the pregnancy from the size of the udder.

Housing is prepared by treating the floor with slaked lime or spraying with an agricultural disinfectant, which is also used for the feed barrier, feed troughs etc. Ewes are normally housed at the end of this month to give them time to adjust to their new quarters and altered diet. They accept hay readily if they have been receiving hay in the field.

Chapter 8   Late Pregnancy and Lambing

Fig. 8.1 Ewe and lambs in a mothering-up pen. *Photo: M.K. Collard*

Late pregnancy

During the last six weeks of pregnancy the sheep are fed with care *(See Chapter 6)*, and disturbed as little as possible. The *booster vaccination* against clostridial diseases is given *(see Chapter 5, Vaccinations)*, the exact time varying with the brand. This can be carried out with little stress if the sheep are penned tightly.

Out-wintered ewes are brought into a sheltered paddock near the farm, and before lambing straw bales are placed on the grass to provide shelter for new-born lambs. Lambing pens with water buckets are erected in a sheltered corner of the field for ewes with multiple births or sick lambs.

Where ewes are housed lambing pens are placed in the most convenient position, usually around the perimeter or within easy reach of the exit.

Sick bay

Before lambing begins a *sick bay* should be prepared. This should contain:

• a couple of pens suitable for sheep with lambs, and ideally a comfortable corner with a power supply, containing a warming box for hypothermic lambs, and facilities for feeding weak lambs with a stomach tube.

The Medicine Chest

This should be stocked not later than two weeks before lambing. Special ear tags should be ordered many weeks in advance Not all the items will be needed every year. The chest should contain:

General:
• Thermometer
• Syringes and needles
• Plastic disposable gloves
• Electrolyte solution for ewes & lambs, and soluble dextrose for an energy boost.
• Torch.
• Record cards and pen.
• Agricultural disinfectant for disinfecting lambing pens between occupants, mild disinfectant for use when lambing.

For the ewes:
• Wormer and dosing gun.
• Foot clippers.
• Lubricating fluid.
• Plastic prolapse retainer (inter-uterine support). If this is not successful call the vet to insert stitches. In the first year the following items are for use with a helper or after attending a lambing course:
• Lambing cords.
• Calcium borogluconate MP (added magnesium and phosphorus), for the treatment of calcium deficiency, pregnancy toxaemia or hypomagnesaemia when the diagnosis is questionable. If a ewe has had to be lambed she will need an injection of antibiotic.

For the lambs:
• Tincture of iodine for treating navels.
• Rubber rings and applicator for docking and castrating.
• Ear tags and applicators.
• Aerosol colour spray for identifying the ewes with their lambs.
• Warming box: this can be constructed at home, *(See Chapter 10, under Warming Methods).*

For poorly and orphan lambs:
• Bottles and teats.
• *Milton*, or a similar preparation, for disinfecting feeding equipment.
• Colostrum, either frozen or a couple of sachets from the farm supply shop; this can be fed in a bottle to a new born orphan lamb that can suck.
• A stomach tube and 50ml. syringe are needed to feed colostrum to a lamb that cannot suck. (Only to be carried out after instruction or by a helper).
• Ewe milk replacer - this is milk powder for orphan lambs. It is best to have ready a small quantity in a plastic bag in case of emergencies - hopefully it will not be needed.

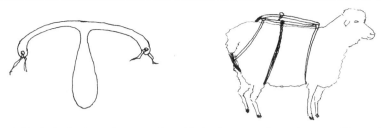

Fig 8.2 Left: A plastic prolapse retainer. Right: A rope prolapse harness. To use the latter:
•Take the centre of a 3m length of cotton rope and place it on the ewe's front legs. Bring the ends up each side and tie securely over the spine, between the shoulders.
• Bring both lengths together along the backbone, pull taut and tie the lengths together (not the ends) over the backbone, above the hips.
• Stand behind the ewe and separate the two lengths of rope. Take one length to the right of the tail, down across the vulva, under the back left leg and up to the backbone, pull taut and tie to the other length of rope lying over the spine.
• Repeat this procedure with the other length of rope in the opposite direction, pull taut and tie to the other length of rope lying over the spine.
• Check that the truss is taut and tie again if necessary. The rope may stretch a little so the harness will need checking from time to time to make sure that it is still stretched tightly over the vulva.

• A recovery unit for young lambs is needed. This can be constructed out of paper lined cardboard boxes surrounded by bales, with a *heat lamp* suspended *4ft. above the backs of standing lambs,* to avoid overheating. *Infectious cases and all abortions should be treated away from the main housing.*

• A pen in an airy but sheltered location should be prepared for *orphan lambs.* They will need a bucket of water, a milk bar (a rack holding bottles or a bucket fitted with teats), a small hay rack, a container at mouth level for a few lamb nuts, and a straw bale, centrally situated, to play on.

• A medicine chest as detailed on page 49.

Prolapse of the cervix
This is not uncommon in very late pregnancy in well fed ewes bearing twins. When the protruding cervix appears to be about the size of a large grapefruit a plastic prolapse retainer, obtainable from farm suppliers *(Fig. 8.2),* can be inserted and kept in place by tying to the fleece. If the prolapse re-appears or is very large the vet must be called.

Behaviour of the lambing ewe
Pre-lambing behaviour
Luckily the lambing behaviour of ewes does not vary from breed to breed, but unfortunately it does vary considerably between individuals. This is surprising in view of the fact that from the beginning of labour till 24 hours after birth hormonal changes are largely in control.

The first sign that the pregnancy is coming to an end is given by the udder which starts to swell as it fills with colostrum during the week before birth. Unfortunately this can vary from slightly longer than a week to only a few hours. If it is not possible to pen all the ewes individually before lambing, choose those that were covered first and those with swollen udders, because these will lamb first.

When birth is three hours or so away about two thirds of ewes will become restless, but this period of unease can vary from about eleven hours to ten minutes! The ewe will get up, lie down and get up again many times over. She will often paw the ground, and may bleat, lick her lips or flick her tongue in and out. When she has started to lose fluid she will lick the ground on which it has been spilt, and if another ewe is lambing nearby, she will lick the neighbour's fluid and try to lick the neighbour's lamb. She may attempt to steal the lamb and sometimes, especially if the neighbouring ewe is engaged in producing a twin, she will succeed. This behaviour may lead to the death of the neighbour's lamb, because the ewe may lose interest in it when she produces her own, and if the separation has lasted some time the real mother may not recognise her lamb, and reject it.

This situation is most likely to arise in a housed flock or where large numbers of ewes are held in a restricted area. Individual penning solves this problem *(Fig. 8.1)*, but even so care has to be taken because a ewe may lick a neighbour's lamb through the rails of the pen and thereby attract it. To prevent a lamb becoming confused place a board between the pens until the lamb has *mothered-up* properly.

Another indication of the coming birth is given when the ewe separates herself from the flock and goes into a quiet corner. Where sheep are housed but not individually penned, it is advisable to construct several small pens along the edge of the building so that lambing ewes can retreat into them. When labour starts, about 50% will use the pens. This reduces the awkward task of penning newly lambed ewes intent on returning to the birth site. Out-wintered ewes will chose elevated, protected and sheltered birth sites, often near walls or fences.

Once the lamb has entered the birth canal the ewe will lie down, hold her head upwards and towards her tail, and start straining. During this period she will lie down and get up frequently. After 20-30 minutes the water bag may appear hanging out of the vulva but can burst inside so that only the fluid is discharged. Birth usually takes place after a further 20-30 minutes with the front feet and nose appearing first *(Fig. 8.3)*. The progress of the lamb down the vagina is a very important part of the birth process because vaginal stimulation leads to strong maternal responses in the ewe. Therefore it is wrong to pull the lamb from the ewe unless there is a very good reason.

Fig. 8.3 Position of the lamb's head in a normal birth. Note that the soles of the hooves point downwards.

Primitive breeds and hill breeds tend to be in labour for a shorter time and have fewer complications than more developed breeds, such as the meat breeds. Multiple births last longer in total but the birth of the first lamb is quicker than for a single, and subsequent births are very much quicker, an interval of 20 minutes between twin births being normal. First time lambers usually have a somewhat longer labour. Occasionally they will wander around, or even run about, with half the lamb projecting and banging on the ewe's back legs. Eventually the ewe continues with the birth process and the lamb is not harmed.

In other cases an extended labour is a cause for concern. An internal examination should be carried out when labour has exceeded 90 minutes, or exceeded 30 minutes after the appearance of either the water bag or the liquid from it. If the lamb appears to be lying in the correct position and the ewe is not exhausted, she can be left for another 30 minutes before she is lambed. The ewe will require help without further delay when the lamb is lying correctly (head and front feet first) but is too large for her to deliver, or when the lamb is lying incorrectly. When only the head, only one leg or a tail is showing it is clear that the lamb is lying incorrectly and that the ewe will have to be lambed. Dead lambs must be removed. To see if the lamb is dead, or very weak, put a finger in the lamb's mouth to see if it can suck.

Do not lamb a ewe until you have had instruction, both theoretical and practical. Wear disposable gloves, use plenty of lubrication and keep the ewe, yourself and your working area, as clean as possible. Plenty of warm soapy water is necessary and a paper sack placed under the ewe is a great help. Do not use disinfectant unless it is very mild and well diluted, as chemicals can harm the vagina and uterus. Proceed slowly and gently. It is usually possible to correct the position of the lamb's front legs within five minutes but first make sure, by feeling along the limbs, to which lamb they belong, and if they are front or back legs.

If within ten minutes no progress has been made in delivering the lamb, call the vet. The ewe will need an injection of antibiotic following internal examination or intervention, in case an infection has been introduced.

Supervision during lambing may interrupt the contractions of the uterus; however, the better the supervision during lambing, the more lambs will be saved. This is particularly important in prolific flocks where some twins or triplets may be very small and require attention. It may be necessary to remove the firstborn for a while to encourage the ewe to bond with lambs born later. Sometimes a lamb suffocates because the ewe does not remove the membrane from its nose, and occasionally she can kill one by lying on it. Supervision can reduce these deaths. Particular attention is paid to first time lambers as they may have difficulty in adapting to motherhood. To avoid startling sheep at night leave the lights on and talk to your sheep as you approach them.

Behaviour of the ewe following birth - 1 The sensitive phase
During this period, which lasts about 24 hours, maternal behaviour is mainly controlled by hormones. Their effect is exceedingly strong immediately after birth but wanes rapidly. At this stage the ewe recognises its lamb almost entirely by smell, later, in the second period, the maintenance phase, sight and hearing are increasingly important.

When the lamb drops onto the straw the movement of the ewe in turning to inspect her lamb causes the umbilical cord to tear; the tearing prevents a haemorrhage. She will then start licking away the membrane covering the lamb's head, and within two minutes the lamb shakes its head and takes its first breaths. The ewe continues to lick the lamb vigorously, which aids circulation and helps to dry the coat. Following birth the normal bleat of the ewe changes to a much deeper tone called a 'rumble'. When this distinctive sound is heard in the flock, it is an indication that a ewe has lambed recently.

When a ewe is exhausted after a difficult birth, or if a second lamb is born very quickly after the first, the shepherd should clean the membrane away from the head of the new-born, and place it in front of the mother, so that she can lick away the birth fluids without having to stand or to leave the firstborn. When the lamb stands and the ewe will help it find her udder by giving it gentle nudges in the right direction. By the time a twin is born it has started suckling. When lambing is completed the ewe starts to eat hay with a good appetite, and drinks large amounts of water to allow for lactation and to replace the body fluids lost during birth.

After the ewe has lambed, contractions of the uterus continue in order to expel the placenta or afterbirth. This may happen within minutes of the birth but often takes a few hours. The ewe may eat the afterbirth; even so it is usually easy to see that it has come away because liquids will be seen on the floor of the pen. The ewe must be given fresh bedding and the afterbirth removed as soon as possible. Occasionally part of the afterbirth can be seen hanging out of the ewe. Trying to remove it can seriously damage the uterus, therefore an injection of antibiotic should be given and the ewe given plenty of time to continue the process.

Fig. 8.4 Agricultural colleges and training groups offer courses in sheep handling and lambing. *Photo: Otley College.*

Following birth - 2 The maintenance phase

This period lasts from 24 hours following birth to weaning. The importance of the smell of the lamb as a method of recognition continues, and, for the first few weeks, the ewe will smell around the lamb's tail before she lets it suckle.Very soon, as she begins to graze further away from her lamb, the sound of its bleat and its appearance become increasingly important. The ewe recognises her lamb's voice and looks for it when it bleats. If she cannot see the lamb but can hear it, she becomes distressed and runs about looking for it, even rushing past it in agitation.

For the first few days following birth the ewe and lamb remain less than a metre apart from one another, and sleep lying together. By the second half of the first week the lamb will leave the mother for short periods to play with other lambs. This does not disturb the ewe but if the lamb bleats she goes to it, and will suckle it at any time. During the second week the ewe grazes further away from the lamb. This has the effect of reducing the frequency of suckling; she also starts to limit its duration by walking away. For the first three to four weeks the ewe will go to the lamb when it bleats but after that will only go part way and bleat for the lamb to come to her. When grazing, the distance between the ewe and lamb increases during the first month, but decreases again as the lamb seeks to keep close to the mother. Measurements have shown that for 75% of the time a lamb grazes within 2 metres of its mother. When ewes are kept in feral or semi-feral conditions, as is the case with mountain sheep, the relationship of the ewe lamb and the mother does not fade, and ewes of the same family will graze to-gether in the same area for their whole lives. This makes it possible to keep mountain flocks together without fencing. In a feral state ram lambs leave their mothers to form *bachelor groups*, and only rejoin the ewes at mating time.

Chapter 9   Caring for Lambs from Birth to Marketing

The care of lambs is the responsibility of the ewe *(Fig. 9.1).* In most cases ewes are devoted mothers and nourish and care for their lambs without problems. The main task of the shepherd is to provide good nourishment for the ewe and a healthy environment for the ewe and her lambs.

Day 1. Navel treatment, suckling, penning

When the lamb has struggled to its feet the ewe concentrates on licking its rear end, which helps push it in the direction of her udder. Lambs find their first drink by following the heat gradient along the underside of the ewe and by nosing about to find bare flesh. This method results in a fruitless investigation of the underside of the ewe's front legs, but the lamb soon moves towards the warmer back area, where it is also attracted by the smell of the wax on the teat. Mountain and primitive lambs can be expected to stand in under twenty minutes and are usually sucking in half an hour. Lowland lambs may take longer.

Treatment of the navel

The first task following a normal birth is to disinfect the navel. This is carried out as soon as the ewe has licked away the major part of the membranes. Tincture of iodine B.P. is recommended because it contains iodine, which is an excellent disinfectant, and alcohol, which not only disinfects the cord but dries and shrivels it, preventing further infection. This treatment is important because the cord is certain to come in contact with the bedding, and the blood vessels in it are an easy route for infection to enter the lamb's internal organs. The iodine should be kept in a very small jar which can be pressed onto the lamb's belly to submerge the entire cord and the surrounding area. A cord that trails on the ground will require shortening to about two inches. The cord is held between the fingers of both hands at two inches from the body, and slowly pulled apart. A haemorrhage may result if the cord is cut, and if only one hand is used the pull on the body wall may cause a rupture. Torn ends heal quickly and should be treated immediately with iodine, as described above.

Suckling

The second task of the shepherd is to ascertain that the lamb is receiving milk when it is sucking, and no lambs should be left until this has been done. The

Fig. 9.1 The care of the lambs is the responsibility of the ewe. *Photo: Laura Densmore*

udder is felt, to make certain that it is emptying; milk is drawn from both teats and blocked teats cleared by gentle manipulation. An udder which feels hard is not emptying, and this can lead to mastitis. To make sure that a lamb is getting milk, and not just sucking a blocked teat or a bit of wool, it is held up by the front legs and the stomach felt to see if it is distended with milk, or flat and empty.

The importance of the first milk (known as colostrum) cannot be overestimated. Not only does it contain large quantities of nutrients, but also all the antibodies which the ewe has produced naturally, or which we have induced her to produce by vaccination. The first twelve hours or so of life is the only period when lambs are able to absorb the antibodies from the gut into the bloodstream. After this time only the antibodies which prevent gut infections are of use. After eighteen hours the colostrum turns to ordinary milk, and a lamb which has not already received a sufficient amount (about 2 pints or 1 litre) is open to infection.

Penning

Where large numbers of sheep are housed it is advisable to pen the ewe and lamb in a mothering-up pen as soon as the lamb has been licked clean. Penning aids in the development of the maternal bond and prevents mis-mothering (another ewe stealing the lamb). Penning is achieved by holding the lamb by its fore-legs, slightly above the ground, with the navel pointing towards the ewe, and then retreating backwards, very slowly, into a freshly strawed pen. The ewe usually follows the lamb without difficulty, but she may return to the birth site, and the procedure will have to be repeated. First-time lambers are more likely to do this than experienced ewes. Where a few sheep are kept in a large space, or where lambing takes place outside, penning may be delayed until the lamb has started to suck.

Day 2. Castration, tail docking and identification

These procedures may be carried out on lambs over 24 hours of age, but should be delayed when the lambs are small, appear weak, or are from multiple births. Good sized twins can be castrated, etc, from two days of age, and triplets from three. The rubber ring method is preferred for both castration and docking, *but is only legal in the first week of life.*

Castration

Male lambs that are to go for slaughter at about four months need not be castrated, because they will not be sexually active by this age, and entire lambs grow more quickly than castrates. Lambs that are unlikely to finish (not be ready for the butcher), or are to be sold as store lambs, should be ringed. To castrate a lamb it is convenient to sit on a bale with the lamb sitting up on its rear on one's lap, with all four legs sticking out in front. This position enables one to hold the lamb against one's body with the left arm, and to use the fingers of the left hand to press the base of the abdomen gently, to prevent the testicles retreating from the scrotum into the abdominal cavity. The right hand is free to operate the instrument which places the ring over the neck of the scrotum. The ring cuts off the blood supply causing the scrotum to shrivel and fall off. Following castration some lambs show considerable discomfort for up to an hour, while others (in my experience the smaller ones), may be affected for only a matter of minutes.

Docking

Docking the tail is necessary to avoid problems with blow-fly. While docking it is comfortable to sit on a bale with the lamb on one's lap. The front legs should hang down on the left, the back legs on the right. The left arm presses the lamb against one's body, while the left hand stretches out the tail, and the right hand applies the rubber ring. Eventually the end of the tail shrivels and drops off *(Fig. 9.2)*. Docking is unnecessary on short-tailed primitive breeds. *It is illegal not to leave sufficient tail to cover the anus in males and the vulva in females.*

Identification

This may be by ear-tags, colour marking, or both. Normal ear-tags tend to get pulled out of the soft ears of young lambs, and colour marks are soon indecipherable, but some way has to be found of re-uniting lambs that get separated from their mothers, so it is probably safest to use both methods together. Special small tags are available for young lambs but need replacing with normal tags.

Fig. 9.2 Ewe and lamb. Note the lamb's tail shrivelling below the docking ring.
Photo: Martin Lynch.

Meconium

This is the name given to the first faeces. This sticky, dark substance sometimes blocks the anus. It must be washed away with warm water because an attempt to pull it away can damage the skin. Faeces produced later are softer and bright yellow, and only occasionally cause a blockage.

Releasing the lambs

Any problems with young lambs are likely to arise within the first week; this should be kept in mind when arrangements for release are made. Housed ewes with young lambs can be released for a day or two into a large pen with several other ewes, or into a yard or a small sheltered paddock, before they are introduced to a large open field with large numbers of other ewes and lambs. Where foxes are a problem it may be advisable to bring the sheep indoors for the first few nights. Sheep which have lambed outside will have done so in the most sheltered paddock available, and should be kept in that paddock, or in another sheltered field, for the first week. Extra shelter can be provided by placing straw bales in the field for the sheep to use as windbreaks. The best time for release is as early in the day as possible and after the ewes have been fed. This avoids the risk of lambs becoming separated from their mothers in a large, strange, dark field, or of the ewes abandoning the lambs while they search for feed.

Feeding and worming

The feeding of ewes and lambs post-lambing is covered in *Chapter 6*. Worming is described in *Chapter 5*, and a worming programme is given in the Husbandry Calendar in *Chapter 4*.

Vaccinations

Vaccination against *Pasteurella* and *Clostridial diseases* is usually carried out at ten weeks, and the booster injection four to six weeks later. The exceptions are lambs that are due to go for slaughter at sixteen weeks because normally they will be protected until that time, and lambs in flocks where there is a known risk from pasteurella or one of the clostridial diseases where earlier vaccination is recommended. Your vet will advise you as to the appropriate date.

Hoof care and prevention of blowfly strike

Lambs are included when these tasks are carried out because lambs' hooves grow surprisingly fast and need clipping, and the effect of blowfly strike on a lamb is very serious and it may die.

Weaning

The date of weaning must be at least eight weeks before the ewe is to return to the ram, and preferably several weeks earlier, to give plenty of time for her to recover condition. Lambs lose condition when weaned, so are given the best grazing, or perhaps some supplementary feeding. Lambs very close to finishing are best left with the ewe until they are ready. Weaning is a stressful period for the lambs so husbandry tasks should be avoided, and the lambs left in the field to which they are accustomed, with the ewes being removed from them.

Marketing

Lambs can be sold through the local market. This is not very satisfactory if the breed is not known locally, and for the inexperienced it is not easy to judge when the lamb has achieved the optimal weight and conformation. Another possibility is to sell your lambs through a local Livestock Marketing firm who will send out a *grader*. He will visit your flock regularly after the first lambs achieve a stipulated weight, mark those he considers ready for the abattoir and arrange for their collection. You will receive notification from the abattoir of the grades the lambs have achieved, and payment from the firm a couple of weeks later. If the lambs are to be kept for home consumption you will need to find a local butcher or abattoir who carries out this service. Members of the *Rare Breeds Survival Trust* may be able to join their marketing scheme.

Chapter 10   Problems at Lambing

Resuscitation

Some lambs may be born with a beating heart but do not start breathing. This may be because the lamb is premature, has suffered from lack of oxygen during birth, or is just slow and starts to breathe after a minute. Obviously, when a lamb is not breathing, immediate action is required. After checking that the airways are clear, you can tickle the nostrils with a straw, give the lamb an energetic rub-down with a towel, or grasp the lamb above the hocks and give it a good swing round, using the whole length of the arm. If the lamb does not breathe after a couple of swings, give up. Do not use mouth to mouth resuscitation as this only inflates the stomach.

Rejection

Sheep are such devoted mothers that it is disturbing to watch a ewe rejecting her lamb. When a second twin is born a long time after the first, the ewe may refuse to take any notice of it, and it may be necessary to remove the firstborn until she has taken to the second. Sometimes, especially when the birth has been difficult, it is enough to give the ewe a deep bucket containing concentrate, and the lamb will attach itself to the udder while the mother is occupied. Once the ewe lets the lamb suck there is no further problem. Unfortunately, ewes are very stubborn, and if rejection continues she must be placed in an adoption pen in which she is restrained by the neck, can eat and drink, but is unable to turn around to push the lamb away. If the lambs feed satisfactorily, the ewe can be released after 48 hours into a small pen, but even if she accepts the lambs she will need watching for a few days. When the ewe kicks the lambs away or rejects them when she is released, they must be bottle fed.

Fostering

In large, prolific, housed flocks, fostering is not only used in emergencies but also as a management tool. Constant supervision makes it possible to remove a triplet soon after birth, and give it to a ewe which has just had a stillborn lamb or a single. The smallholder with far fewer sheep is lucky if his ewes lamb within hours, let alone within minutes, so that fostering is a more difficult procedure with a lower success rate.

When a lamb needs to be fostered at birth, and a ewe with a newborn single or dead lamb is available, the foster mother's birth fluids are rubbed into the lambs' coat, especially on the head and the rear, the lamb's legs are tied together and it is given to the foster mother to lick clean Leave the lamb for a while, then release the legs, and watch until it is suckling.

When a lamb is up to 6 hours old, it is put in a clean dustbin with the foster mother's lamb, the foster mother's afterbirth and any other birth fluids. The two lambs are left in the bin for 30 minutes at a distance from the ewe. Then the bin is placed in the pen with the ewe but the lambs are not released and given to her about another 30 minutes. By this time both lambs should smell alike to the ewe and she should allow the foster lamb to suck. Should she reject the lamb, it is removed, fed and hand reared.

Feeding with a stomach tube

A lamb that is too weak to suck but can hold up its head when lying on its stomach, can be fed *colostrum* through a stomach tube *(See Chapter 8, under Medicine Chest)*. Tube feeding is also used when a healthy lamb is not getting colostrum because the mother has only one teat functioning, has no milk, or has died when no foster mother is available. Immediate bottle feeding is not advisable, as a lamb will find it harder to accustom itself to the foster mother's teat should a foster mother become available, and weaker lambs may get pneumonia if milk from the bottle gets into the windpipe. Feeding with a stomach tube is not difficult but *it is wise to ask someone to demonstrate the technique*. After use, the tube and syringes should be washed and disinfected immediately, and kept in an antibacterial solution (*Milton* or similar) until the next feed.

Feeding newborn lambs

A newborn lamb requires an absolute minimum of three feeds per day at eight hour intervals. On this regime each feed consists of 50 ml per kilo of bodyweight. For a 3 kg lamb this means 3 feeds of 150 ml each, amounting to a total of 450 ml per day. A 4 kg lamb would require 600 ml per day. It is far better to divide the total feed into 4 or 5 feeds per day given at regular intervals, and this is a necessity for lambs that are small or weak.

An average lamb feeds from the ewe 14 times per hour in the first hour, 10 times in the second, half hourly by 8 hours, and hourly at the age of one week. Bags of ewe milk replacer have feeding instructions printed on the bag.

Lambs cannot be fed if they are unable hold up their heads or are unconscious. They will need an injection of glucose into the body cavity, carried out by a vet or an experienced shepherd.

Hypothermia

The normal temperature of a lamb is between 39⁰C and 40⁰C. (102⁰F - 104⁰F). When the temperature is between 37⁰C - 39⁰C the lamb is suffering from moderate hypothermia, and below 37⁰C the lamb has severe hypothermia. Problems are

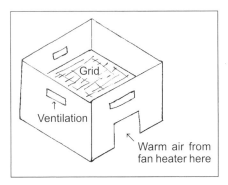

Fig. 10.1 A Warming Box

indicated by any of the following: the lamb does not run to the ewe when disturbed, stands with the head hanging down, has the front and back legs close together and the back slightly arched, or is spending most of the time lying down. The lamb must be inspected and its temperature taken, preferably with a digital thermometer which is easy to read. Unfortunately, hypothermia, due either to exposure or starvation, is a common problem in lambs. Clearly lambs born outside are likely to suffer from exposure, and for this reason may be too weak to suck properly and will die of hypothermia from both causes.

A moderately hypothermic lamb should be dried well, given a feed through a stomach tube and returned to the ewe in a sheltered pen. If it does not start to feed from the ewe it must be fed again with the stomach tube, and then put in a box under an infra-red lamp placed 4ft (120 cm) above it, *not lower* to avoid scorching. When the lamb has recovered it may be returned to the ewe but if this is so late that she rejects it, the lamb should be hand reared because weak lambs are difficult to foster.

Severely hypothermic lambs must be warmed. The best method is with warm air and a thermostat.

When the lamb is **less than five hours old** it should be dried, warmed till its temperature exceeds 37°C., fed with a stomach tube, and returned to the mother. If it has siblings, the other lambs should be removed at the same time and returned with the weakling to avoid its rejection.

A lamb **over five hours old** that can hold up its head should be tube fed first, then dried, warmed, fed again and returned to the ewe. If it cannot hold up its head it must be warmed before feeding. Lambs that do not improve, and lambs with a high temperature, 41°C. and over, may be suffering from other conditions, very possibly infectious, and the vet should be consulted without delay.

Warming methods

Before warming, lambs must be well dried with a towel to prevent heat loss through evaporation. The traditional method of warming a lamb by the kitchen fire is inexact, as is the use of an infra-red lamp, which may cause skin burns as well as overheating the lamb. The best method is to use a thermostatically controlled warming box with a lid, in which the lamb lies upon a grid about half way up the box, and warm air is blown around it. It is possible to make a similar construction using a strong box, a grid supported on bricks (I use the grid from the barbecue!), a room thermometer and a domestic warm air heater, which is placed outside a hole in the bottom of one side of the box (*Fig.10.1*). A close watch must be kept to see that the temperature in the box remains between 35⁰C. and 37⁰C, and that the lamb's temperature is taken regularly, so that it can be fed and returned to its mother as soon as it reaches 37⁰C.

Hand Rearing

Weak lambs should be place in a box with an infra-red lamp as described above. Other lambs should be placed in a sheltered pen with plenty of straw. In very cold weather an infra-red lamp may be hung above the most sheltered corner. Feeding may be by bottle or a lamb bar.

Bottle feeding involves warming the milk to blood temperature and feeding at regular intervals.

A lamb bar can be a rack holding several bottles or a bucket with many teats projecting from it. When the lambs are put on the teats every 20 minutes or so, they start drinking from the lamb bar by themselves in considerably less than a day. Lambs feed frequently, taking small amounts, so it is not necessary to heat the milk. The lamb bar is cleaned and re-filled daily.

Fig. 10.2 Three prize-winning Southdown ram lambs. Note the halters used for shows.
Photo: Surrey County Show.

Chapter 11   Wool, Shearing and Selling

The British commercial sheep farmer is a producer of meat lambs, and because he receives a low return for his wool has little interest in it. This is not true of most smallholders who value their sheep as wool producers. Some breed sheep with interesting fleeces, and achieve a reasonable return by selling wool to hand-spinners. Sheep keepers who have no interest in wool can avoid shearing by keeping the Wiltshire Horn breed which has a sparse hairy coat that moults in the spring.

The British Wool Marketing Board

The marketing of British wool is controlled by the *British Wool Marketing Board* in Bradford, which represents over 80,000 wool producers. Owners of more than four sheep are obliged to register with the Board and, with two exceptions, sell their wool through it. The exceptions are:

• the sale of wool direct to handspinners.

• the sale of the wool of a few of the rarest British sheep breeds.

The collection of wool is arranged throughout the country by agents of the Board, which are firms known as *wool staplers*. In the early spring the firms deliver the *wool sheets* (big bags in which the wool is to be packed), to the producers, and collect them after shearing. Before the wool is sent to Bradford it is graded according to quality, which determines the amount the Board will pay. Deductions are made if the wool is dirty; suffers from vegetable contamination; contains pieces of baler twine; includes black hairs or is 'coloured', meaning yellowish. Naturally coloured wool (black, grey or brown) achieves a low price, although there are special grades for a few naturally coloured breeds, such as the black and white Jacob and the black or grey Herdwick.

The *BWMB* publishes an annual list of the prices they are paying for the various grades, and distributes this to producers. There are a large number of grades, many of which bear the names of sheep breeds. It is important to realise that these names only indicate the type and quality of the wool. When a grader feels that a Shetland fleece does not correspond with the grade of that name, he will enter it in another grade.

The *BWMB* has an interest in improving and promoting British wool. Their free *Ram Fleece Assessment Service* provides expert information about the quality of the wool of a ram to be used for breeding, and the Board encourages and supports training for new shearers and for those wishing to improve their skills. Information is available from *BWMB. (See Reference Section).*

Fig. 11.1 A mixed flock of rare and primitive breed ewes kept for their speciality wool. *Photo: Katie Thear*

Shearing

The appropriate time to shear

In the lowlands and warm areas of the country, shearing takes place towards the end of May or in the first half of June, depending on the weather. In the north and on the hills it may be necessary to wait until July.

Preparing the sheep for shearing

Wool must be both dry and clean for shearing, and the process is more comfortable for both sheep and shearer when the sheep have not eaten beforehand and are less likely to soil the fleece.

Ideally the flock should be brought into a clean building or yard in the late afternoon of a sunny, breezy day when the wool should be bone dry. They should be provided with water but no feed and definitely no bedding, and should be shorn as early as possible on the following day.

When they are returned to their lambs, the lambs will not recognise their mothers immediately, so it is wise to put the whole lot together in a small paddock where they can sort themselves out - a very noisy process.

Fig. 11.2 Shearing time. *Photo: Katie Thear*

Preparing the building or yard

Plenty of hurdles should be available to pen the sheep securely. It is convenient if a pen containing a few sheep, four or five, is situated close to the shearing area, and has a single pen leading from it, so that a single sheep is always ready for the shearer as soon as the last has been shorn.

Shearing is done on a clean surface, a wooden floor which is easily swept is excellent, but a large piece of old carpeting or a tarpaulin will suffice. The area is enclosed with hurdles to prevent half-shorn sheep escaping into the flock *(Fig. 11.2)*.

The shearer needs a power source close at hand, and a nail or hook up on the wall above his head, on which he can hang the motor, enabling the cable to hang down out of the way of the sheep. A large, smooth table is placed close by so that the shearer can throw the fleece onto it, and the wool sheet is hung within easy reach.

Fig. 11.3 Newly shorn sheep.
Photo: Katie Thear

The shearing and packing procedure

Four people are needed for this to run smoothly but three will suffice. One person is needed to shear, one to keep the shearer supplied with sheep, one to roll and pack the fleeces, and preferably one to let out the shorn sheep and help control difficult animals. It is possible to combine the last two jobs.

When the shearer throws the fleece onto the table a considerable amount of loose dirt falls away. The packer spreads out the fleece skin-side down, (a few Hill Breeds are packed starting with the outside of the fleece touching the table surface), and with the long side towards him. Any soiled parts (the *daggings*) are pulled off and thrown onto a heap. Next the packer folds the long sides of the fleece to the middle, and then rolls it up tightly, starting from the rear end. When he arrives at the neck he stretches the wool out a little way and tucks it well down into the centre of the fleece, to prevent the roll unwinding. This method of presentation is required by the *Wool Board*. The fleece is then placed in the wool

Fig. 11.4 Sheep should only be carried in a purpose-built vehicle or trailer. *Photo: Katie Thear*

sheet. Care must taken to keep coloured wool away from white wool. Fleeces destined for sale to hand spinners are kept separate. They need unrolling at a later date for careful inspection before bagging and labelling (see final paragraph in this chapter). The *Wool Board* requires daggings to be packed separately and pays very little for them.

Shears

Electric clippers are used by professional shearers and are expensive.

Hand shears are not difficult to use but shearing with them is a slow process. They are adequate for a few sheep and, if the operator is skilled, for a small flock.

The shearing process

This is one of many country crafts that looks quite simple but is a skilled operation. The shearer must be able to hold a frightened sheep securely against his body with one hand, while operating the shears with the other. He must be able to alter the position of the sheep when necessary, and hold the skin taut to avoid cuts. *Would-be shearers are well advised to go on a shearing course.* In many areas there are shepherds who are willing to shear a few sheep during summer evenings or at weekends, and make a practice of shearing small flocks. Local sheep keepers will know of them.

The most common shearing method today is a one man operation with the sheep sitting up on its rump for the first part, and lying on the ground for the second, but many other methods have been used in the past. Whichever method is used, care must be taken to avoid the penis of rams and the teats of ewes. Cuts are treated with an anti-bacterial spray.

When the owner of a few sheep has observed how shearing is done, there is no reason why he should not use hand shears and any shearing method that suits him. Some sheep keepers ask another person to help hold the animal, while some quiet animals can be tethered and shorn standing. Traditionally a few of the Longwool breeds are shorn in this way, starting at the backbone, and shearing the two sides separately.

Shearing with hand shears should be done carefully and methodically. If one cuts too far from the skin this must be tidied up after the fleece has been removed. Spinners hate 'double-cuts', because they result in very short pieces of wool in a fleece with a longer staple.

Wool for crafts

Preparation and sale: Fleeces for hand spinners should be unrolled and inspected to make sure they are clean, free of vegetable matter and without any cotted areas. *Cotted* wool is wool that has felted on the sheep and will not comb-out for spinning. Dirty, rough wool from the rear end will have been removed already, but since most spinners have no use for coarse, straggly belly wool, this is best removed from the edge of the fleece. To test for possible breaks in the fibre, a small lock of wool should be pulled from the fleece, stretched between the hands and tugged sharply. If it breaks or if a narrowing of the fibres is detected, the fleece must be rejected. Checks in wool growth are likely to occur in the fleeces of sheep that have been ill or have suffered sudden alterations in their condition, probably due to the demands placed on them by lambing or poor feeding.

Packing and labelling: Packing and labelling for private customers should be carried out with care. Labels should list the breed and colour, the fleece weight, price per kilo, price of the fleece, and whether organo-phosphate free dips have been used. It is advisable to provide scales so that customers can weigh the wool.

One of the many joys of owning a small flock is the opportunity it gives to handle and appreciate wool. One is no longer surprised that wool became *"The sovereign merchandise and jewel of this realm of England"* (Ordinance of the Staple), and this is not all. We are in debt to the wool and cloth merchants for building the most outstanding of our parish churches and manor houses, and we owe even more to the sheep which, by grazing our countryside throughout the year, have given us the openness of the mountains in Scotland, Wales and the Lake District; the wide landscapes of the Dales, Downs, Wolds and Moors; and the well-tended appearance of our lowland pastures.

Reference Section

Government Regulations and Codes of Practice Concerning Sheep

Under this heading I have only sought to make clear the areas in which regulations and codes of practice apply. I have attempted to name the authorities enforcing the implementation of regulations and suggest sources of information, but cannot accept responsibility for errors or omissions. Regulations and Codes of Practice are constantly being changed and up-dated. This is largely due to changes in the policy of the British Government and European Union, reaction to health concerns, and the introduction of new medication and agricultural methods. Responsibility lies with sheep-keepers to advise themselves of current regulations by contacting the appropriate authorities. Sheep-keepers can keep abreast of new developments in the sheep industry and possible new regulations, by reading the agricultural press or belonging to an organisation such as the *NSA (National Sheep Association*, The Sheep Centre, Malvern, Worcs. WR13 6PH. 01864 892661).

Although this area may appear confusing, and a minefield for the ill-informed, the object of regulation is to protect our customers, our sheep and ourselves, and therefore should be approached with as much understanding as we can muster.

Registration

This is the first requirement when you start to keep sheep. Registration, which is obligatory even if you own only one sheep, is through the local *Animal Health Office*, which is part of the *Ministry of Agriculture, Fisheries and Food,* and is situated in the local *MAFF* Office. You must supply your name and address, and notify this office within one month if any of these details change.

Movement records

Any movement of sheep to or from your holding must be recorded within 36 hours of the movement taking place. Confusingly, the officers responsible for supervising this legislation are *Animal Health Officers*, attached to a Department of the County Council (often *Trading Standards*), or, in some areas of Scotland, the Police. The *Animal Health Officer* should be able to provide a *MAFF (Ministry of Agriculture, Fisheries and Food)* booklet *Sheep and Goat Identification,*

Records and Movement. A Guide to the Legal Requirements (Jan. 1996), and a book in which one can record the appropriate details. The movement record must contain:

• The date of the movement.
• The identification marks of the sheep involved.
• The total number of sheep moved.
• The holding from which the sheep are moved.
• The holding to which the sheep are moved.
• The total number of sheep on your premises in January each year.

The record must be retained for three years from the end of the year in which the last entry is made.

When sheep are moved they must be accompanied by a *Sheep and Goat Movement Document* unless they are moving:

• between holdings in the same occupation
• to and from common grazing
• for veterinary treatment, dipping, shearing, or to a show, provided the sheep are due to return to the original holding.

The Movement Document must be given to the occupier of the holding of destination and kept by him for six months. The Animal Health Officer of the County Council provides copies of the Movement Document.

If sheep are sold without moving them on or off a holding the following details must be recorded: the date of the sale, the number of animals sold, their identification marks and the name and address of the purchaser.

An *Animal Transport Certificate* is required, and must accompany the sheep, if they fulfil one or more of the three following requirements:

• if they are being moved over 50km
• if the sheep are not your own
• if the internal measurement of the livestock compartment exceeds 3.7m.

This document must be kept by the transporter for 6 months following the movement. The Animal Health Officer of your County Council provides copies of this certificate and also an *Animal Transport Guide for Farmers and Hauliers.* Only healthy animals may be transported. Ewes that are likely to give birth, or have done so in the preceding 48 hours, and young lambs where the navel has not yet healed, may not be transported.

Identification

At present the regulations given below are in force, but new regulations concerning the identification of sheep within the UK are under discussion.

• Sheep for export must be identified with an ear tag or tattoo which should contain 'UK', the flock mark and an individual animal number.

• The tag should include a 'P', 'S' or 'G' between the flock mark and individual number.

• The *flock mark* is the number allocated by your local *MAFF Animal Health Office* to identify the flock. It is not the same as the *Agricultural Holding Number* which is allocated by *MAFF* to identify the area of land on which the holding is situated. At present when sheep are moved within the UK they can be identified with a management tag, tattoo or colour mark, ear notch, horn brand or leg band. If animals are moving from a market they must be identified by their lot number.

Vehicles for transporting animals

There are many regulations covering this area, many of which are mainly concerned with professional hauliers. Information can be obtained from the *Animal Health Officer* of the County Council. Livestock should only be carried in a purpose built vehicle or trailer, constructed and maintained in accordance with the *Welfare of Animals (Transport) Order 1997*. Bedding should be provided for the sheep, and, if the vehicle is large, it should contain divisions for small groups of sheep or single sheep.

Trailers weighing up to 750kg MAM (maximum authorised mass) are not required to have brakes, but the towing vehicle must have a kerb-side weight of at least twice the actual in-use weight of the trailer. In effect this means that a small car may tow a small trailer containing a couple of small sheep, but risks exceeding the permitted weight with more or heavier animals. A useful guide *Towing and the Law* is published by the *Society of Motor Manufacturers and Traders Ltd.*, Forbes House, Halkin St., London, SW1X 7DS.

Welfare of sheep and shepherd

MAFF produces a booklet *Codes of Recommendations for the Welfare of Livestock - SHEEP.* It is obtainable from local *MAFF* offices or *Animal Health Officers* of the County Council. Areas covered include management, feed and water, pregnancy and lambing, artificial rearing and housing. Specific regulations prohibit *"short-tail docking unless sufficient tail is retained to cover the vulva in the case of female sheep or the anus in the case of male sheep"*, and the use of a rubber ring without an anaesthetic for castrating and docking, other than in the first week of life. An anaesthetic is also required when using other methods to dock or castrate rams over three months; castration over this age must be performed by a vet. Only a vet is permitted to dehorn or disbud a sheep, with the exception of the trimming of the insensitive tip of an ingrowing horn which could cause pain or distress if untreated.

Sheep farmers need to hold a *Certificate of Competence in the Safe Use of Sheep Dips* before they can buy any sheep dips. Anyone who disposes of used dip must have an *Authorisation* (written consent) to do so and will be obliged to pay a registration fee, and an annual fee. Applications can be made to the *Environment Agency* (local Environment Agency Officer (0645 333111) or the *Scottish Environment Protection Agency* (01786 457700). Contractors with sheep showers treat sheep, and, since they take away the used liquid, this is likely to be the best method for a smallholder. Outbreaks of blowfly can be prevented with *pour-on* medication, which is sprayed on the wool with a small hand-held sprayer.

The welfare of the shepherd is the concern of the *Health and Safety Executive* which has recommendations on protective clothing for shepherds when dipping sheep.

Health

Animal Medicines Record Book

This is used to record animal medicine purchases, batch numbers, dates, usage, withdrawal periods and veterinary visits, and should be available for inspection by *Ministry Officers, Animal Health* and *Veterinary Inspectors*. I find it useful to keep all the bills from my vet as they record details of the medication supplied.

Unused medicines

These must be disposed of safely. The best method is to return them to the vet, along with used hypodermic needles and syringes. To make the needles safe they can be stuck into a cork.

Notifiable Diseases

These are very serious diseases, most very rare, and must be reported to the police or a Ministry vet at the local MAFF office. They are listed in veterinary books. Sheep which are itching badly should always be reported to your vet, as the animal may be suffering from **Scab**, in which case one is obliged to dip the flock in a Scab-approved dip and it is forbidden to move the flock unless for treatment or slaughter. *ADAS* publish a leaflet on scab, P593 *Sheep Scab*. The address of the local ADAS office is obtainable from *MAFF*.

Scrapie is a brain illness with symptoms similar to Scab. The causal agent resembles the BSE agent, and if the disease is diagnosed the sheep must be destroyed. Current recommendations relating to the avoidance of Scrapie transmission, mean that shows can only mix sheep of Scrapie-monitored and non-monitored status between 1 May and 31 August, and will not be accepting in-lamb ewes or ewes that have lambed less than 30 days before the show.

Disposal of carcases and slaughter

The *Movement Book* should record the removal of a dead sheep to a knacker's yard or hunt kennels, which are the best places to dispose of carcases.

Sheep sent to a butcher or abattoir for slaughter can be rejected if they are dirty. Sheep which are to be slaughtered for consumption after the eruption of the first adult teeth must be slaughtered in the presence of a vet and have the spinal cord removed. This may make the slaughter of an older animal more expensive.

Wool

Owners of more than four sheep must register with the *Wool Marketing Board*, Oak Mills, Station Rd., Clayton, Bradford BD14 6JD, and, with a few exceptions, must sell their wool through them. Exempted is the wool of a few of the rare breeds of British sheep, and wool sold to handspinners.

Sheep Annual Premium

This is a subsidy paid to sheep farmers who have registered with the Ministry of Agriculture and received, or purchased or leased, a *Quota Allocation*. This is the number of ewes for which one is entitled to receive subsidy. For lowland farmers the subsidy is called *Sheep Annual Premium*. Farmers in the LFAs (less favoured areas) receive a larger premium, while upland farmers receive an additional *Hill Livestock Compensatory Allowance (Sheep)* for breeds suited to the environment. Several conditions apply to sheep farmers receiving subsidy. Special records must be kept, the flock can be inspected at any time, and the number of sheep receiving subsidy must be kept on the holding (or other sites which have been declared) for a one hundred day period from the beginning of February until mid-May. This is known as the *retention period*.

Insurance

I know of no specific regulations covering sheep, but owners should seek advice as to third party liability. Clearly the owner of a holding which is crossed by public footpaths, or where access to the fields is from a public highway, has more problems than a hill farmer living half a mile up a dirt track, with gates every few hundred yards. It is wise to seek advice from an agent specialising in rural insurance. The *NFU (National Farmers Union) Mutual* can be contacted through your local *NFU* office. The NFU also runs an organisation, *NFU Countryside*, which offers members a free *Legal Assistance Helpline*.

As I have stated in the first paragraph, this section is only intended to help new sheep keepers contact the authorities responsible for regulating the sheep industry, and indicate the areas in which regulations apply. The information given is correct as far as I am aware, but I must reiterate that I cannot accept responsibility for errors or omissions.

Bibliography

Publications

The Behaviour of Sheep, J.J. Lynch, G.N. Hinch, D.B. Adams. CAB International and CSIRO Australia.

British Sheep. National Sheep Association, Ninth Edition 1998.

The Modern Shepherd, Dave Brown and Sam Meadowcroft. Farming Press.

Practical Lambing and Lamb Care, F.A.Eales and J. Small. Longman Scientific and Technical.

Practical Sheep Dairying, Olivia Mills, Thorsons Publishing Group.

Practical Sheep Keeping, Kim Cardell. The Crowood Press.

Sheep Ailments, Eddie Straiton. Farming Press.

The Veterinary Book for Sheep Farmers, David C. Henderson. Farming Press.

Country Smallholding Magazine. Monthly articles on the care of a small flock and on sheep breeds. Tel: 01799 540922. Fax: 01799 541367. E-mail: info@countrysmallholding.com

Country Smallholding Books & Videos. Supplies all those currently in print by post. For a free catalogue contact as above.

Organisations

National Sheep Association, The Sheep Centre, Malvern, Worcs WR13 6PH. Tel: 01684 892661.

Rare Breeds Survival Trust, National Agricultural Centre, Stoneleigh Park, Warks CV8 2LG. Tel: 024 7669 6551.

The British Wool Marketing Board, Wool House, Roydsdale Way, Euroway Trading Estate, Bradford BD4 6SE. Tel: 01274 688666.

International Sheepdog Society, Chesham House, 47 Broomham Road, Bedford MK40 2AA. Tel: 01234 352672

British Coloured Sheep Breeders'Association, Pool Farm, Grosmont, Abergavenny, Gwent NP7 8HU. Tel: 01873 831328.

Suppliers

The local branch of a farm supply firm will be able to provide you with feed, and medication which is not on prescription. They stock hurdles and electric netting which are satisfactory for the smallholder, but the footbaths, hayracks etc, are likely to be too large and are best purchased from a specialist supplier. The addresses given below are of firms that cater for smallholders or supply homeopathic remedies. They understand the problems of the small producer and are willing to give advice on the telephone.

Feeds

Allen and Page, FREEPOST: ANG 4981, Shipdham, Norfolk, IP25 7ZZ. Helpline for dealing with feed problems 01362 822908.

W.H. Marriage and Sons Ltd, Chelmer Mills, New Street, Chelmsford, Essex, CM1 1PN. Phone 01245 354455 for further information.

Both these firms stock feeds which are based on organic principles.

Equipment

Small Acres Supplies, Ty Mawr Uchaf, Llanerfyl, Welshpool, Powys SY21 0JE. Tel: 01938 820495.

Ascott Smallholding Supplies, Anvil House, Dudleston Heath, Ellesmere, SY12 9LJ. Tel: 01691 690750.

Oxmoor Smallholder Supplies, Harlthorpe, Selby, E. Yorks YO8 6DW. Tel: 01757 288186

Homeopathic remedies

Ainsworth's Homeopathic Pharmacy, 36 New Cavendish Street, London, W1M 7LH. Tel: 020 7935 5330. Orders by return of post. *Homeopathy, The Shepherd's Guide*, is a booklet available from the same address.

Homeopathy for Sheep and other Animals, D. M. Harrison, Homeopathic Pharmacy, Ffynnonwen Natural Therapy Centre, Llangwyrfon, Aberystwyth, Dyfed, SY23 4EY. Tel: 01974 241795. Orders by telephone.

The age of sheep

When buying sheep their age should be determined by their teeth, for teeth cannot lie. *(See Chapter 4).*

When describing sheep over four years of age, the number of times it has been shorn is stated eg. *five shear, six shear.*

Sheep can live to ten years and over if they receive good grazing and concentrates when necessary. It may be necessary to help a very aged ewe after lambing by supplementary feeding her lambs with a bottle two or three times a day.

> *"A four-shear ewe is in her prime.*
> *A five-shear ewe in lambing time*
> *As good; six past she will decline.*
> *Ere seven come, away with thine.*
> *Yet many men with profit keep*
> *In warme low grounds and pasture sweet*
> *An eight, nine or ten shear sheep".* (Traditional)

Glossary

Blowfly Green bottle flies and some other types of fly, which lay their eggs on dirty or sweaty wool, and whose maggots make their way down to the sheep's skin and eat into the flesh.

Broken mouthed An older sheep with missing teeth.

Britch wool Coarse wool from the rear end.

Cast sheep A sheep lying on its back and unable to rise, also known as **rig-welted**. Alternatively an old sheep only suitable for the butcher.

Claws or **Cleats** The two halves of the sheep's hoof.

Colostrum Thick milk containing antibodies, produced in the hours following birth.

Colour marker Spray or crayon used to identify sheep which have been treated.

Concentrates Pelleted feeds made largely from cereals.

Condition score A method of assessing the nutritional and health status by feeling the backbone.

Cotted wool Wool that has felted on the sheep.

Creep feed Tiny pellets for young lambs, creep feeder a feeder with sliding bars which prevents the ewes having access to the feed once the lambs have become accustomed to it, creep gate a barrier constructed to admit lambs only.

Crimp Waviness in the wool fibres.

To **Crutch** To clip wool away from the tail area.

Cudding The chewing of regurgitated feed; the **cud** is the lump of regurgitated feed.

To **Cull** The selection of sheep that are to be sold or slaughtered due to a defect or advanced age; the **cull** is the occasion on which this is carried out.

Dagging shears Small shears for removing the dirty wool from the back end of the sheep, can be used for hand shearing for those with small hands. The **daggings** are the dirty bits of wool that have been shorn off.

To **Dock** To shorten the tail of lambs.

To **Dose** To administer a worming preparation. The **dosing gun** is a large syringe calibrated to give exact doses of wormer.

Draft ewes Hill ewes sold or transferred at over four years old to softer lowland pasture.

Ear tags Identification tags fixed to the ear.

Elastrator Instrument for applying docking and castration rings.

Feed barrier Barrier incorporating troughs and/or hay racks, forming the front of a sheep shed, or internal divisions between pens holding up to thirty sheep.

Finished lamb Lamb ready for the butcher.

Flat rate feeding Method of feeding equal portions of feed throughout the four weeks preceding lambing.

Flushing The practice of increasing the fertility of ewes by improving nutrition before mating.

Foot bath Shallow container for medicated water, designed to fit in a pen or race.

Foot shears Small, strong shears used to trim the feet.

Gimmer Ewe between first and second shearing.

Handling system Arrangement of hurdles and gates; used to control the flock during dosing, foot treatment, etc.

Hog, hogget Full male and female sheep between weaning and first shearing.

Hyperthermia A dangerously high temperature.

Hypothermia A dangerously low temperature.

Improved pasture Pasture that has been ploughed and re-seeded.

Kemp Very coarse woollen fibres.

Mastitis Infection of the udder.

Mis-mothering A ewe stealing another's lamb.

Mothering-up The development of the ewe-lamb bond during the first hour of life.

Nuts Pelleted feed.

Orf A highly infectious and serious condition which can be transmitted to humans.

Pink eye (ovine conjunctivitis) A very infectious eye condition.

Polled Hornless.

Pour-on Blow-fly preventives which are sprayed onto the fleece.

Prolificacy The average number of lambs that a ewe, flock or breed will produce.

Race A corridor the width of one sheep, used when handling.

Raddle Colour applied to the ram during mating to mark covered ewes.

Scouring (the scours) An attack of diarrhoea.

Scrapie A very serious disease, initially causing irritation.

Shearling A sheep which has been shorn once, i.e. a sheep aged about fifteen months.

Sheep Scab A very serious disease, initially causing irritation.

Stepped-rate feeding A method in which rations are regularly increased before lambing and decreased at the same rate afterwards.

Stocking rate The number of sheep that can be carried per acre.

Store lambs Lambs being kept to be fattened for the butcher.

Strike Blowfly attack; a **struck sheep** is one suffering from strike.

Teg Female between weaning and shearing.

Terminal sire Ram of a meat breed, used on other breeds to produce meat lambs.

Theave Ewe between first and second shearing.

Tup Ram; **tup lamb** is a ram lamb; **tupping** is mating.

Unimproved pasture Pasture that has not been ploughed and re-seeded

Wether Castrated male.

Withdrawal period Length of time prescribed between medication and slaughter.

Wool grease Lanolin.

Wool sheets Large bags for packing shorn fleeces.

To Worm To administer wormer.

Zoonoses Illnesses which can be transmitted from animals to humans.

Index